Oh! My Grammar ①

CEDU BOOK

Unit Components

• LISTEN & CIRCLE

Fun and authentic context helps students to easily understand how to use the grammar in real life.

• GRAMMAR POINT

Students can learn the target grammar through easy-to-read tables and colorful illustrations with clear examples.

• LET'S PRACTICE

Various kinds of exercises and drills are designed to develop students' understanding of the grammar they learned. These will also gradually encourage students to apply the forms accurately.

• LET'S WRITE

The extended writing activity encourages students to use the language more productively in a variety of contexts.

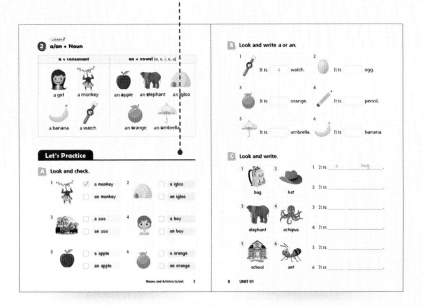

• REVIEW

The review sections help students to recall the language they learned in the previous three to four units. They also allow students to evaluate their understanding of the grammar.

• MINI TEST

The mini test is a cumulative review incorporating the previous seven to eight units. Students will be able to differentiate the grammar points they learned and use them appropriately.

FREE GRAMMAR LESSON

Friendly and detailed grammar audio lessons in Korean are provided to help students comprehend the grammar points more easily.

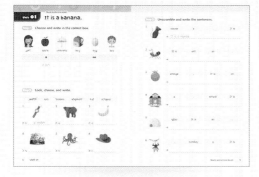

WORKBOOK

Each unit consists of three steps of writing exercises. These are designed to develop students' sentence building skills. They can reinforce their writing skills and gain confidence by completing the exercises.

Contents

Nouns & Pronouns

Be Verbs

Demonstratives & Possessives

Present Simple

Modal Verb *can*

Wh- Questions & Prepositions

Nouns and Articles (a/an)

It is a banana.

✦ **Listen and circle.**

a zoo   a banana   an apple   a monkey   an elephant

1 Nouns

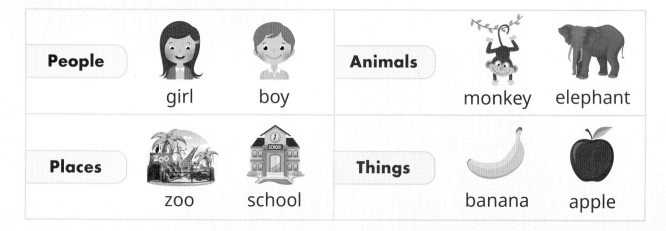

| People | girl | boy | Animals | monkey | elephant |
| Places | zoo | school | Things | banana | apple |

2 *a/an* + Noun

a + consonant	an + vowel (a, e, i, o, u)
a girl **a** monkey	**an a**pple **an e**lephant **an i**gloo
a banana **a** watch	**an o**range **an u**mbrella

Let's Practice

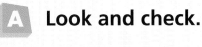

A Look and check.

1
☑ a monkey
☐ an monkey

2
☐ a igloo
☐ an igloo

3
☐ a zoo
☐ an zoo

4
☐ a boy
☐ an boy

5
☐ a apple
☐ an apple

6
☐ a orange
☐ an orange

B Look and write *a* or *an*.

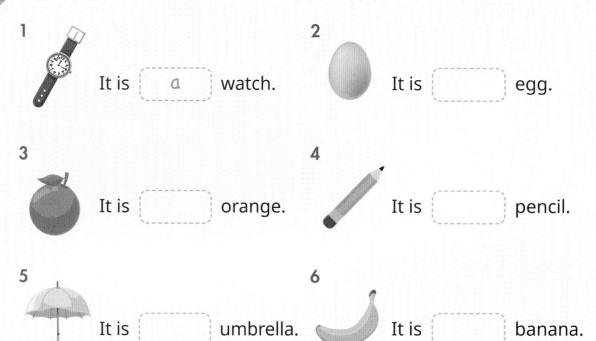

1 It is [*a*] watch.

2 It is [   ] egg.

3 It is [   ] orange.

4 It is [   ] pencil.

5 It is [   ] umbrella.

6 It is [   ] banana.

C Look and write.

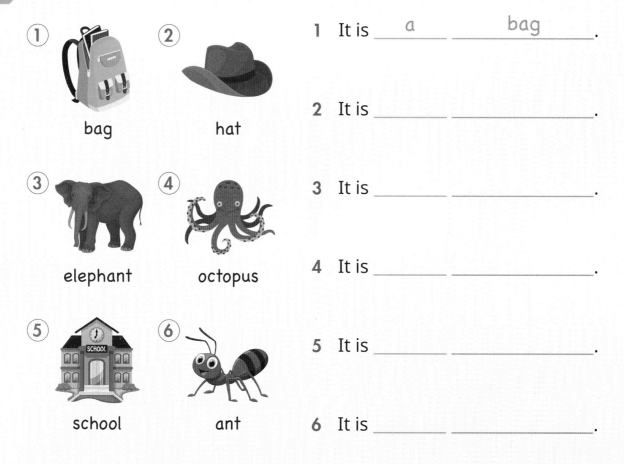

1 bag
2 hat
3 elephant
4 octopus
5 school
6 ant

1 It is _____ *a* _____ *bag* _____.

2 It is _____.

3 It is _____.

4 It is _____.

5 It is _____.

6 It is _____.

✏ **Look, find, and circle.**

pencil   watch   igloo   umbrella   banana

✏ **Look at the picture above and write.**

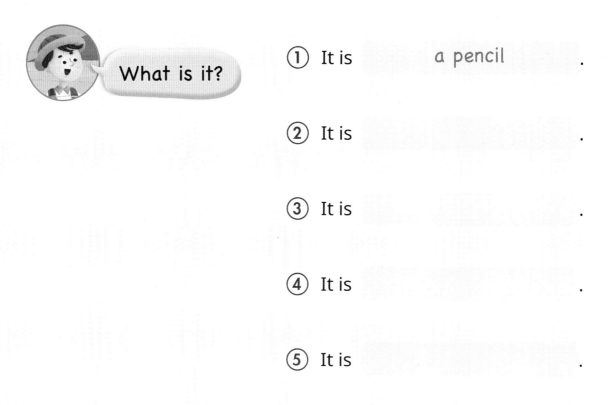

What is it?

① It is   *a pencil* .

② It is   .

③ It is   .

④ It is   .

⑤ It is   .

Plural Nouns

They are books.

✦ **Listen and circle.**

| chairs | dishes | books | boxes |

1 Noun + s

	Singular		Plural	
-s	a book	a chair	book**s**	chair**s**

2 Noun(-ch/-sh/-s/-x) + *es*

	Singular		Plural	
-es	a wat**ch**	a di**sh**	wat**ches**	di**shes**
	a bu**s**	a bo**x**	bu**ses**	bo**xes**

Let's Practice

 A **Look and circle.**

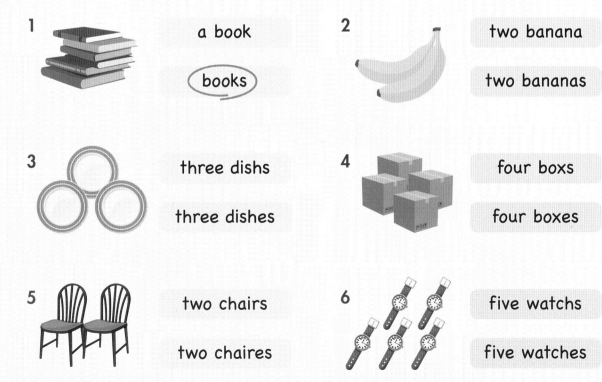

1. a book
   books

2. two banana
   two bananas

3. three dishs
   three dishes

4. four boxs
   four boxes

5. two chairs
   two chaires

6. five watchs
   five watches

B Look and match.

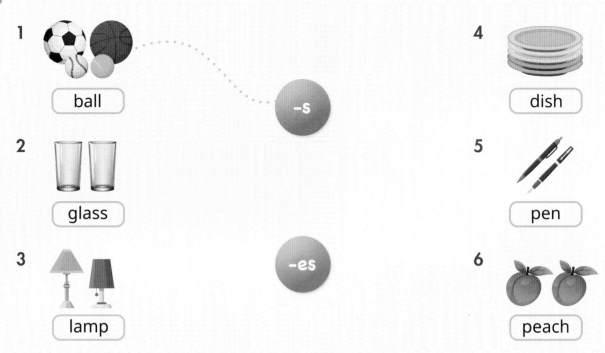

1 ball

2 glass

3 lamp

-s

-es

4 dish

5 pen

6 peach

C Look and write.

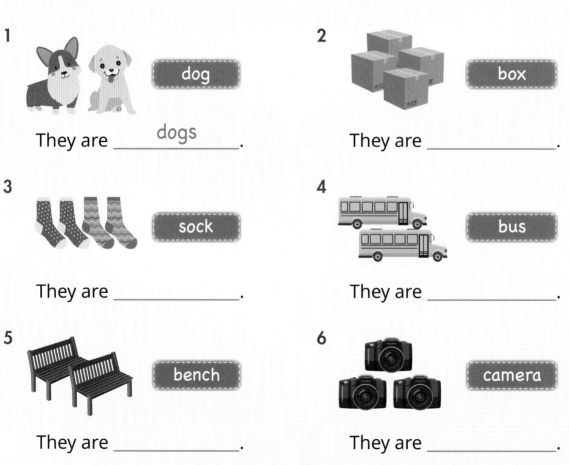

1 dog

They are _____dogs_____.

2 box

They are _____.

3 sock

They are _____.

4 bus

They are _____.

5 bench

They are _____.

6 camera

They are _____.

Look and guess. Then, choose and write.

cat	watch	cup	brush	bus

 What are they?

① They are _____cats_____.

② They are _____.

③ They are _____.

④ They are _____.

⑤ They are _____.

Subject Pronouns

I am Danny.

✦ **Listen and circle.**

I am Danny.
It is my house.

He is my father.
She is my mother.

They are my dogs.

We are a family.
I love my family.

| I | it | he | she | they | we |

LESSON ✏️

1 **Places, Animals, and Things**

it	they
It is a house. **It** is a dog. **It** is a tree.	**They** are houses. **They** are dogs. **They** are trees.

2 People

I	you	he	she
 I am Kate.	You are my sister.	He is my dad.	She is my mom.

we	you	they
We are friends.	You are my sisters.	They are my family.

Let's Practice

A Look and match.

1

2

3

we   they   he   it   I   she

4

5

6

B Look, choose, and write.

| you | she | I | it | he | they |

1 _____You_____ are my friend.

2 _____ is a ring.

3 _____ am a student.

4 _____ are houses.

5 _____ is my grandpa.

6 _____ is my mom.

C Choose and circle.

1 **Ann** is my sister.

| He | (She) |

2 **Kitty** is my cat.

| It | They |

3 **Emma and I** are friends.

| I | We |

4 **Eric and Sally** are my cousins.

| We | They |

5 **You and Brian** are students.

| He | You |

✎ **Look and match.**

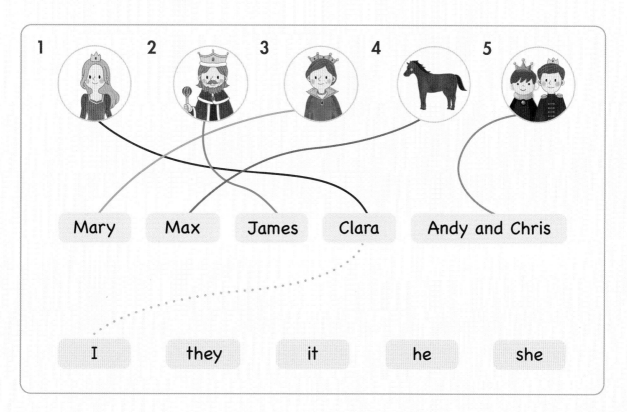

✎ **Look at the activity above. Then, complete the sentences.**

① I'm Clara. _____I_____ am a princess.

② This is James. _____ is my father.

③ This is Mary. _____ is my mother.

④ This is Max. _____ is my horse.

⑤ They are Andy and Chris. _____ are my brothers.

A Look and check.

1.
[✓] a book
[ ] an book
[ ] books

2.
[ ] a igloo
[ ] an igloo
[ ] igloos

3.
[ ] a dish
[ ] three dishs
[ ] three dishes

4.
[ ] a hat
[ ] four hats
[ ] four hates

5.
[ ] I
[ ] you
[ ] it

6.
[ ] he
[ ] she
[ ] they

B Look and circle.

1 It is ⓐ / an zoo.

2 It is a / an ant.

3 It is a cat / elephant .

4 They are boxs / boxes .

5 It is an umbrella / watch .

6 They are lions / liones .

7 They are benchs / benches .

8 They are brushs / brushes .

C Look, choose, and write.

| I | they | he | we | she | it |

1. ___I___ am Bella.

2. _____ is my dad.

3. _____ are shoes.

4. _____ are friends.

5. _____ is my mom.

6. _____ is a shoe.

D Choose and write the singular or plural nouns.

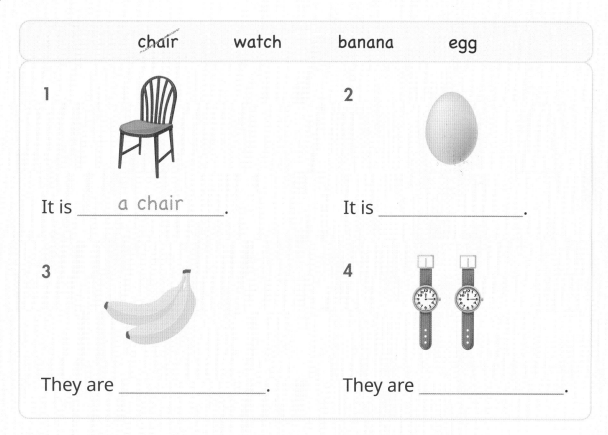

| chair | watch | banana | egg |

1. It is ___a chair___.

2. It is _____.

3. They are _____.

4. They are _____.

E **Look and write.**

1

It is _____a_____ monkey.

2

They are _____.

3

It is _____ apple.

4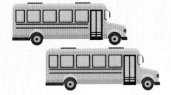

_____ are socks.

5

They are _____.

6

They are _____.

7

It is _____ school.

8

_____ is a king.

9

_____ is a queen.

10

They are _____.

F **Correct the mistakes.**

1  It is <u>a</u> orange. → *an*

2 <u>He</u> is my grandma. →

3  It is <u>a</u> octopus. →

4  They are <u>camera</u>. →

5  They are <u>watchs</u>. →

6 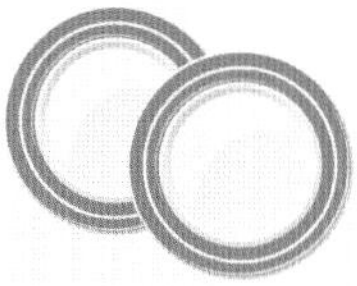 They are <u>dishs</u>. →

7 <u>They</u> is a lamp. →

8 <u>She</u> are girls. →

Julie and I

Unit 05

He is a bus driver.

✦ Listen and circle.

This is Mr. Brown. He is a bus driver.

It is my school.

This is Ms. Stevens. She is my teacher.

We are her students.

he is   it is   she is   we are

LESSON

1 Pronoun + *Be*

Singular		Plural	
I	**am**	We	**are**
You	**are**	You	**are**
He			
She	**is**	They	**are**
It			

I **am** a teacher.

You **are** a student.

He **is** a bus driver.

We **are** teachers.

You **are** students.

They **are** bus drivers.

It **is** a bus.

They **are** buses.

LESSON

2 Short forms

I **am**	⇒	I'**m**
He / She / It **is**	⇒	He'**s** / She'**s** / It'**s**
We / You / They **are**	⇒	We'**re** / You'**re** / They'**re**

Let's Practice

A **Read and circle.**

1 He   am / are / (is)   a teacher.   2 I   am / are / is   a nurse.

3 They   am / are / is   doctors.   4 It   am / are / is   a school.

B **Write the short forms.**

1 **It is** a flower. → It's a flower.

2 **We are** singers. → _____ singers.

3 **You are** my friend. → _____ my friend.

4 **I am** a bus driver. → _____ a bus driver.

5 **She is** a teacher. → _____ a teacher.

C **Look and write.**

1

I __am__ a student.
__I'm__ a student.

2

It _____ a map.
_____ a map.

3

We _____ girls.
_____ girls.

4

She _____ a dancer.
_____ a dancer.

5

They _____ goats.
_____ goats.

6

He _____ a cook.
_____ a cook.

Let's Write

✎ **Look, choose, and complete the sentences.**

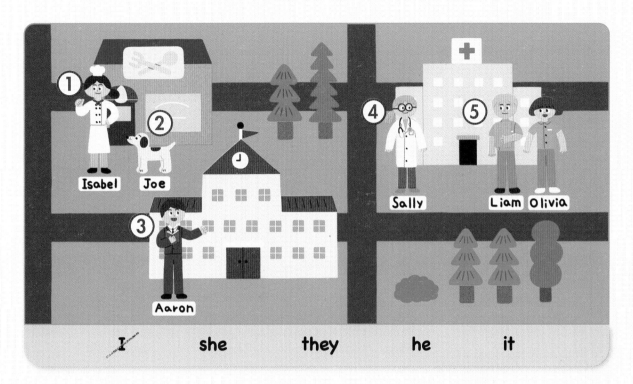

I   she   they   he   it

① Hello, I am Isabel. ____I'm____ a cook.

② This is Joe. _____ _____ my dog.

③ This is Aaron. _____ _____ a teacher.

④ This is Sally. _____ _____ a doctor.

⑤ They are Liam and Olivia. _____ nurses.

Be Verb: Negatives

They are not full.

 05

✦ **Listen and circle.**

am not   is not   are not

 LESSON

1 Pronoun + *Be* + *Not*

Singular		Plural	
I	**am** not	We	**are** not
You	**are** not	You	**are** not
He			
She	**is** not	They	**are** not
It			

I am happy.
I **am not** sad.

You are sad.
You **are not** happy.

She is hungry.
She **is not** full.

We are happy.
We **are not** angry.

It is big.
It **is not** small.

They are small.
They **are not** big.

2 Short forms

I **am not**	⇒	I'**m not**
He / She / It **is not**	⇒	He / She / It **isn't**
We / You / They **are not**	⇒	We / You / They **aren't**

Let's Practice

 Read and circle.

1 She am not / (is not) sleepy.   2 They is not / are not sad.

3 I am not / is not hungry.   4 It is not / are not big.

5 We am not / are not thirsty.   6 He is not / are not a cook.

B Read and circle.

1 He is'nt / (isn't) happy.

2 We are'nt / aren't tall.

3 I'm not / I amn't a student.

4 The bear isn't / aren't small.

5 The teachers isn't / aren't young.

C Look and write.

1

They ___are___ ___not___ big.
They ___aren't___ big.
They're small.

2

She _____ _____ hungry.
She _____ hungry.
She's full.

3

I _____ _____ sleepy.
_____ _____ sleepy.
I'm excited.

4

You _____ _____ happy.
You _____ happy.
You're sad.

✎ **What do they need? Look and match.**

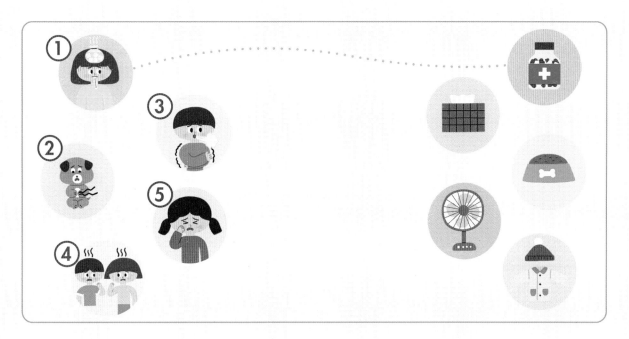

✎ **Look at the pictures above and write.**

① I ____am____ sick. ____I'm____ ____not____ okay.

② It _____ hungry. It _____ full.

③ He _____ cold. He _____ hot.

④ They _____ hot. They _____ cold.

⑤ She _____ sad. She _____ happy.

Is he a cook?

✦ **Listen and circle.**

Is he   Is she   Are they   Are you

LESSON

1 Be Verb: How to make a question

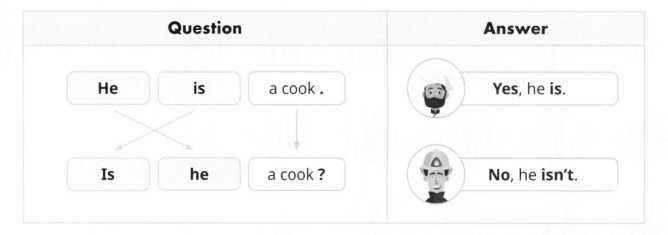

Question			Answer	
He	**is**	a cook .		**Yes**, he **is**.
Is	**he**	a cook ?		**No**, he **isn't**.

2 Be Verb: Question and Answer

	Question	Answer	
Singular	**Are** you ...?	**Yes**, I **am**.	**No**, I'm **not**.
	Is he / she / it ...?	**Yes**, he / she / it **is**.	**No**, he / she / it **isn't**.
Plural	**Are** you ...?	**Yes**, we **are**.	**No**, we **aren't**.
	Are we ...?	**Yes**, you **are**.	**No**, you **aren't**.
	Are they ...?	**Yes**, they **are**.	**No**, they **aren't**.

Are you a doctor?
Yes, I **am**.

Is she a cook?
Yes, she **is**.

Is it a chicken?
Yes, it **is**.

Are you doctors?
No, we **aren't**.
We are nurses.

Are they teachers?
No, they **aren't**.
They are bakers.

Are they chickens?
No, they **aren't**.
They are ducks.

Let's Practice

A Change the sentences to questions.

1 You are a nurse. ➡ [Are] [you] a nurse [?]

2 He is a firefighter. ➡ [   ] [   ] a firefighter [   ]

3 They are doctors. ➡ [   ] [   ] doctors [   ]

B Look, write, and circle.

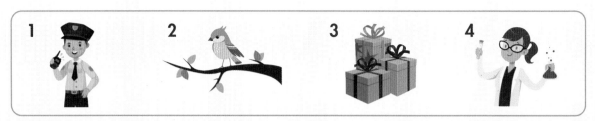

1 ____Are____ you a firefighter?

Yes, I am. / (No, I'm not.)

2 _____ it a bird?

Yes, it is. / No, it isn't.

3 _____ they gifts?

Yes, they are. / No, they aren't.

4 _____ she a cook?

Yes, she is. / No, she isn't.

C Look and write.

1

____Is____ he a baker?

Yes, ____he____ ____is____.

2

_____ they pilots?

Yes, _____ _____.

3

_____ it short?

No, _____ _____.

4

_____ you a doctor?

Yes, _____ _____.

5

_____ they ducks?

No, _____ _____.

6

_____ she happy?

No, _____ _____.

Look and complete the dialogues.

① _____Are_____ you a butterfly?

No, _____ _____. I'm a bird.

② _____ _____ a butterfly? [she]

No, she _____. She's a bee.

③ _____ _____ a butterfly? [he]

No, he _____. He's an ant.

④ _____ _____ butterflies?

Yes, they _____. They're your family!

A Look and check.

1

☐ They is students.
☑ They are students.

2

☐ It is small.
☐ It is not small.

3

☐ Kate is a teacher.
☐ Kate am a teacher.

4

☐ We are angry.
☐ We are not angry.

B Look and match.

1 Is he a bus driver?   No, she isn't.

2 Are you bakers?   No, I'm not.

3 Is she a doctor?   Yes, he is.

4 Are you happy?   Yes, we are.

C Look and write.

1

He __isn't__ sleepy.

__He's__ excited.

2

You _____ a doctor.

_____ a baker.

3

It _____ short.

_____ long.

4

We _____ cooks.

_____ pilots.

5

I ____ ____ hungry.

_____ full.

6

They _____ cows.

_____ horses.

D Read and complete the dialogues.

1 **Q** ____Is____ she a dancer?

A Yes, __she__ __is__.

2 **Q** _____ they sad?

A Yes, _____ _____.

3 **Q** _____ an elephant big?

A Yes, _____ _____.

4 **Q** _____ you a nurse?

A No, _____ _____.

5 **Q** _____ you firefighters?

A No, _____ _____.

6 **Q** _____ Tom a singer?

A No, _____ _____.

Mini Test 1

◆ **Look and check.**

| 1 |  | ☐ It is a umbrella. |
| | | ☐ It is an umbrella. |

2 ☐ They are peachs.
☐ They are peaches.

3 ☐ He is a police officer.
☐ She is a police officer.

◆ **Look and write.**

4

It is _____ school.

5

They are _____.

6

They _____ boys.

7

She _____ sleepy.

8

I _____ a teacher.

9

He _____ sad.

◆ Look and complete the dialogues.

10 _____ you a cook?

Yes, _____ _____.

11 _____ it small?

No, _____ _____.

12 _____ you cold?

Yes, _____ _____.

13 _____ she a pilot?

No, _____ _____.

◆ Find and correct the mistakes.

e.g.

It   is   a   ant.
a   b   c

c ⟶ an

14

They   is   a   monkey.
a   b   c

15

They   are   dish .
a   b   c

16

We   is   friends .
a   b   c

17

They   are'nt   young .
a   b   c

Demonstrative Pronouns

This is a lion.

✦ **Listen and circle.**

this   that   these   those

LESSON ✎

1 **This vs. That / These vs. Those**

2 This / That

This	That
This is a gorilla. This isn't a monkey.	That is a panda. That isn't a bear.

3 These / Those

These	Those
These are bees. These aren't ants.	Those are bats. Those aren't birds.

Let's Practice

A Look and circle.

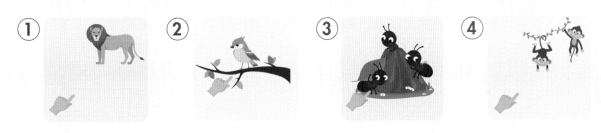

1 This / (That) is a lion.

2 This / That is a bird.

3 These / Those are ants.

4 These / Those are monkeys.

B Look, choose, and write.

this	these	that	those

1

→ _____This_____ is a pencil.

2

→ _____ are apples.

3

→ _____ is a horse.

4

→ _____ are tigers.

C Look and write *this*, *that*, *these*, or *those*. Then, circle.

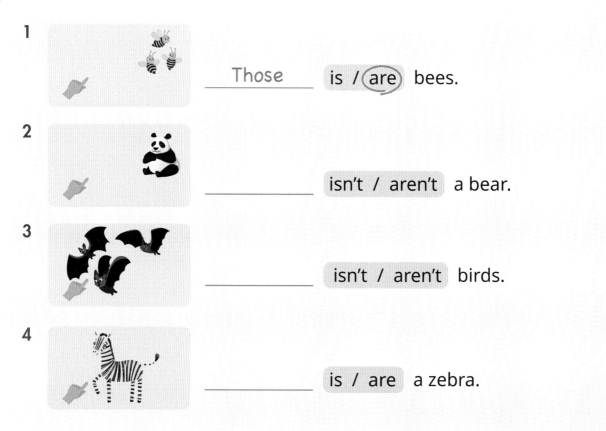

1

_____Those_____   is / (are) bees.

2

_____   isn't / aren't a bear.

3

_____   isn't / aren't birds.

4

_____   is / are a zebra.

✏️ **Look and write with *this*, *that*, *these*, or *those*.**

①   _____This_____ _____isn't_____ a lion.

②   _____ _____ zebras.

③   _____ _____ monkeys.

④   _____ _____ an apple.

⑤   _____ _____ a bird.

Unit 10

Is this a cat?

✦ **Listen and circle.**

1 Questions: This / That

This	That
Is this a dog?	**Is that** a dog?
Yes, **it** is.	No, **it** isn't. It is a cat.

2 Questions: These / Those

These	Those
Are these rabbits?	**Are those** rabbits?
Yes, **they** are.	No, **they** aren't. They are pigs.

Let's Practice

A Look and match.

1 Is that a cat? — Yes, they are.

2 Are those dogs? — Yes, it is.

3 Is this a snake? — No, it isn't.

4 Are these turtles? — No, they aren't.

B **Look and circle.**

1 (Is) / Are (this) / that a dog?

Yes, it is.

2 Is / Are these / those hamsters?

No, they aren't.

3 Is / Are these / those tigers?

Yes, they are.

4 Is / Are this / that a horse?

No, it isn't.

C **Look and write.**

1

Is this a bear?

No, _____it_____ _____isn't_____.

2

Are those pigs?

Yes, _____ _____.

3

Is that a monkey?

Yes, _____ _____.

4

Are these rabbits?

No, _____ _____.

✏ **Look and complete the dialogues.**

①

Is this a chicken?

No, ___it___ ___isn't___.
It is a duck.

②

_____ _____ pigs?

Yes, _____ _____.

③

_____ _____ a rabbit?

Yes, _____ _____.

④

_____ _____ ants?

No, _____ _____.
They are bees. Be careful!

Possessive Adjectives

This is his T-shirt.

✦ **Listen and circle.**

That is my dad.
This is his T-shirt.

That is my mom.
This is her hat.

These aren't my socks.
They are too small.

These are your socks!

| my | his | my | her | my | your |

LESSON

1 **My / Your / Our**

Pronoun	I	you	we	you
Possessive	my	your	our	your

 This is **my** dog.

 That is **your** book.

These are **our** dogs.

Those are **your** books.

2 His / Her / Its / Their

Pronoun	he	she	it	they
Possessive	his	her	its	their

This is **his** T-shirt.

That is **her** dress.

These are **their** bags.

This is **its** toy.

Those are **their** toys.

Let's Practice

A Look and match.

1 you　2 I　3 it　4 she　5 we

my　our　her　your　its

B Look and write.

1 It is ____her____ dress.

2 It is _____ bird.

3 It is _____ school.

4 They are _____ socks.

C Look, choose, and write.

his   their   her   its

1 This is ____his____ cap.

2 That is _____ house.

3 This is _____ car.

4 These are _____ books.

Let's Write

Look and complete the sentences.

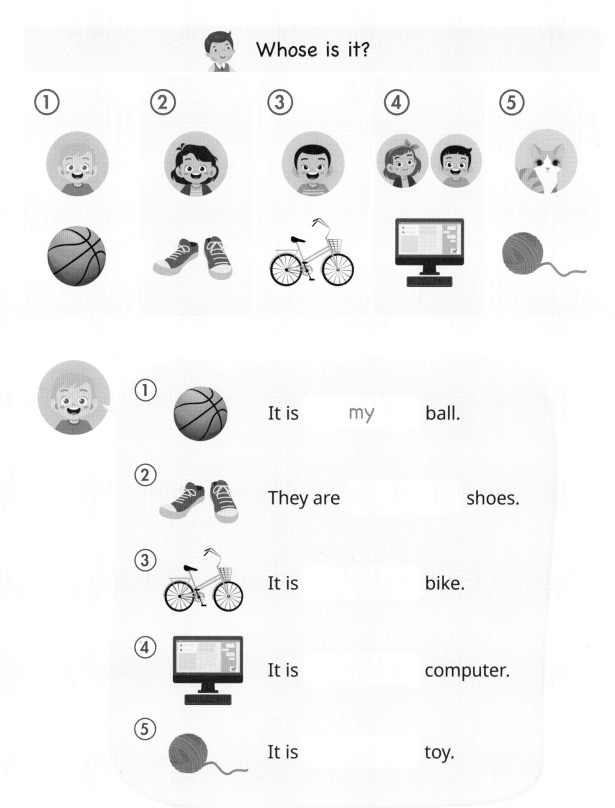

Whose is it?

① ② ③ ④ ⑤

① It is   my   ball.

② They are   shoes.

③ It is   bike.

④ It is   computer.

⑤ It is   toy.

Review 3

A Look and circle.

1 This / (That) is a horse.

2 These / Those are lions.

3 This / That isn't my book.

4 These / Those aren't gorillas.

5 Are these rabbits?
No, they are / aren't .

6 Is that a melon?
Yes, it is / isn't .

B Read and write.

1 That is ____his____ T-shirt.   he

2 These are _____ bikes.   we

3 This is _____ hat.   I

4 Those are _____ socks.   you

C Look and write.

1

__Those__ are apples.

2

_____ is an iguana.

3

Is that a cat?

Yes, _____ _____.

4

Are these lions?

No, _____ _____.

5

_____ those pigs?

Yes, they _____.

6

_____ this a pig?

No, it _____.

D Correct the mistakes.

1 These __is__ birds. These aren't bats. → [are]

2 This is __they__ house. → [ ]

3 That __are__ a turtle. That isn't a fish. → [ ]

4 Those are __she__ notebooks. → [ ]

Mini Test 2

◆ **Look and check.**

1   ☐ This is a zebra.
    ☐ That is a zebra.

2   ☐ These aren't trucks.
    ☐ Those aren't trucks.

3   ☐ The children isn't angry.
    ☐ The children aren't angry.

◆ **Look and write.**

4   She _____ a nurse.   5   They _____ gifts.   6   _____ is a bird.

7   _____ are ants.   8   He _____ a doctor.   9   Those _____ bees.

◆ Look and complete the dialogues.

10 Is the boy thirsty?

Yes, _____ _____.

11 Are these birds?

No, _____ _____.

12 _____ you hungry?

No, _____ _____.

13 _____ this a dog?

Yes, _____ _____.

◆ Find and correct the mistakes.

e.g.

They | are | I shoes.
a | b | c

c → my

14

Those | is | a cow.
a | b | c

_____ → _____

15

It | isn't | we school.
a | b | c

_____ → _____

16

They | are | he books.
a | b | c

_____ → _____

17

This | aren't | a pen.
a | b | c

_____ → _____

Present Simple: Positives

We have dolls.

✦ Listen and circle.

Today is market day.

He **has** a toy car.
She has a yo-yo.

We have dolls.

Wow, they have balloons.
Let's go there!

| ~~has~~ | has | have | have |

LESSON ✏️

1 Have

Have	
I	
You	
We	**have**
They	
The girls	

I **have** a robot.

We **have** robots.

 They **have** toy cars.

 The girls **have** dolls.

LESSON

2 Has

Has	
He	
She	has
It	
The girl	

 He **has** a toy car.

 The girl **has** a doll.

 It **has** a ball.

Let's Practice

A Look and circle.

 ①

 ②

 ③

 ④

1 I (have) / has a balloon.

2 He have / has a robot.

3 You have / has a doll.

4 The cat have / has a toy.

B **Look and write *have* or *has*.**

| 1  | 2 | 3 | 4 |

1 I ___*have*___ a kite.

2 She _____ a teddy bear.

3 Mark _____ a toy truck.

4 Sue and Peter _____ balloons.

C **Look, write, and match.**

1 Emily [has] a doll.

   She [has] a yo-yo.

2 You and Sam [ ] crayons.

   [ ] [ ] notebooks.

3 Brian and I [ ] yo-yos.

   [ ] [ ] toy cars.

4 The puppy [ ] a bowl.

   [ ] [ ] a bone.

✏ **What do they have? Follow the lines and write.**

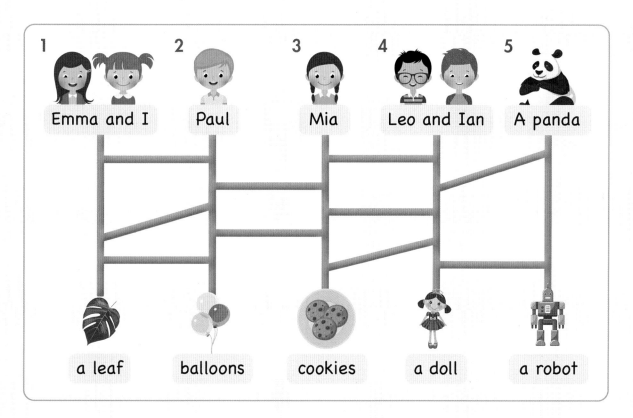

① Emma and I ___have___ ___cookies___.

② Paul _____ _____ _____.

③ Mia _____ _____ _____.

④ Leo and Ian _____ _____.

⑤ A panda _____ _____ _____.

Present Simple: Negatives

I don't have a camera.

✦ Listen and circle.

We are on a mountain.

You have a camera. I don't have a camera.

He has a map. She doesn't have a map.

We have raincoats. They don't have raincoats.

| don't have | doesn't have | don't have |

LESSON

1 Don't Have

Don't Have	
I	
You	
We	**don't have**
They	
Tom and Lia	

don't = do not

I **don't have** a pen.

They **don't have** an umbrella.

Doesn't Have	
He	
She	**doesn't have**
It	
Tom	

doesn't = does not

She **doesn't have** gloves.

Tom **doesn't have** a fork.

A fox **doesn't have** wings.

Let's Practice

 Read and circle.

1 I (don't have) / doesn't have a camera.

2 You don't have / doesn't have an eraser.

3 Lisa don't have / doesn't have a spoon.

4 We don't have / doesn't have raincoats.

5 The tree don't have / doesn't have leaves.

B **What's missing? Write _don't have_ or _doesn't have_.**

① ② ③ ④

1 He [doesn't have] gloves.

2 We [　　　　　] a map.

3 Gina [　　　　　] a scarf.

4 Sally and Peter [　　　　　] a tent.

C **Look and write _have_, _has_, _don't have_, or _doesn't have_.**

A monkey ____has____ arms.

A snake __doesn't have__ arms.

Frogs _____ legs.

Snails _____ legs.

Bees _____ wings.

Cats _____ wings.

A horse _____ a tail.

A gorilla _____ a tail.

Let's Write

✎ **What do they have? Look and complete the sentences.**

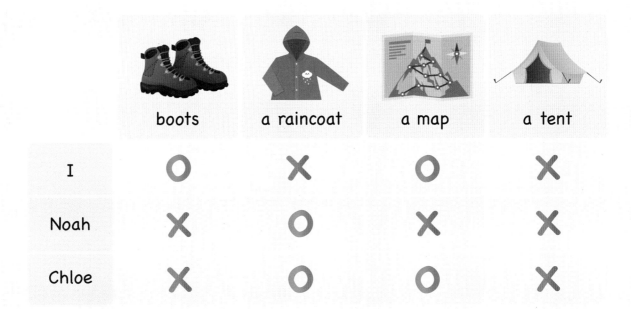

	boots	a raincoat	a map	a tent
I	O	X	O	X
Noah	X	O	X	X
Chloe	X	O	O	X

① We go camping today. I _____have_____ boots.

② I _____ _____ a raincoat.

③ Noah _____ _____ boots.

④ Chloe _____ a map.

⑤ Oh no. We _____ _____ a tent!

Unit 15

Do you have a baseball?

✦ Listen and circle.

do   do   do   don't   does   does

 LESSON

1 Do you have ...?

Question and Answer	
Do you **have** a baseball?	**Do** you **have** bikes?
Yes, I **do.** **No**, I **don't.**	**Yes**, we **do.** **No**, we **don't.**

2 Do we/they have ...?

Question and Answer

Do we **have** a jump rope?

Yes, you **do**.
No, you **don't**.

Do they **have** skateboards?

Yes, they **do**.
No, they **don't**.

3 Does he/she/it have ...?

Question and Answer

Does she **have** a bat?

Yes, she **does**.
No, she **doesn't**.

Does it **have** a fish?

Yes, it **does**.
No, it **doesn't**.

Let's Practice

A Read and circle.

1 (Do) / Does you (have) / has a jump rope?

2 Do / Does he have / has a skateboard?

3 Do / Does a rabbit have / has wings?

4 Do / Does they have / has a basketball?

B **Look and answer the questions.**

I	Amy	Mike	Ryan and Sam

1 Do you have a ball?   ___No___ , I ___don't___ .

2 Does Amy have a bike?   _____ , she _____ .

3 Does Mike have a jump rope? _____ , he _____ .

4 Do Ryan and Sam have a bat? _____ , they _____ .

C **Look and write.**

1

___Do___ they have skates?

No, ___they___ ___don't___ .

2

_____ a frog have a tail?

No, _____ _____ .

3

_____ you have helmets?

Yes, _____ _____ .

4

_____ she have a skateboard?

Yes, _____ _____ .

✎ **Look and complete the dialogues.**

①    Q ____Does____ he ____have____ a bat?

A ____Yes____, ____he____ ____does____.

② Q _____ she _____ a basketball?

A _____, _____ _____.

③ Q _____ he _____ a skateboard?

A _____, _____ _____.

④ 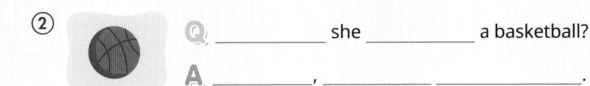 Q _____ they _____ jump ropes?

A _____, _____ _____.

A Read and circle.

1 I ⟨have⟩ / has a jump rope.

2 My sister have / has a robot.

3 Noel and I have / has bikes.

4 They don't have / doesn't have a tent.

5 Snails don't have / doesn't have legs.

6 He don't have / doesn't have a pencil.

B Change the sentences to questions.

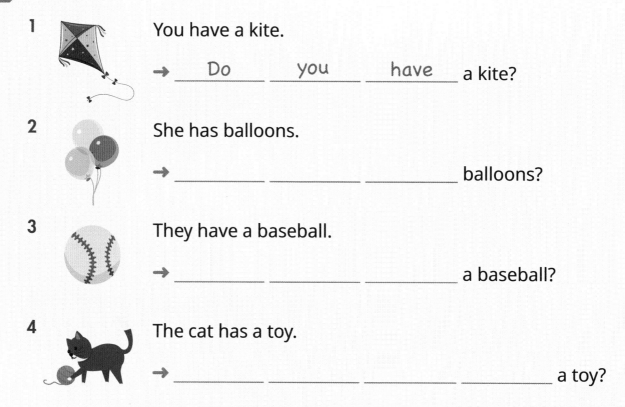

1 You have a kite.

→ ___Do___ ___you___ ___have___ a kite?

2 She has balloons.

→ _____ _____ _____ balloons?

3 They have a baseball.

→ _____ _____ _____ a baseball?

4 The cat has a toy.

→ _____ _____ _____ _____ a toy?

C Look and write.

A kangaroo __has__ a tail.

Bees _____ wings.

A horse has legs.
It _____ _____ wings.

_____ zebras have stripes?
Yes, _____ _____.

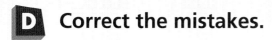

_____ she have a bike?
No, _____ _____.

_____ they have helmets?
No, _____ _____.

D Correct the mistakes.

1 She doesn't <u>has</u> crayons.   →   have

2 A monkey <u>have</u> arms.   →

3 <u>Does</u> snakes have legs?   →

4 They <u>doesn't</u> have a map.   →

Mini Test 3

◆ **Look and check.**

1		☐ That is his dress.
		☐ That is her dress.

2		☐ Tom has a robot.
		☐ Tom have a robot.

3		☐ The girls has dolls.
		☐ The girls have dolls.

◆ **Look and write.**

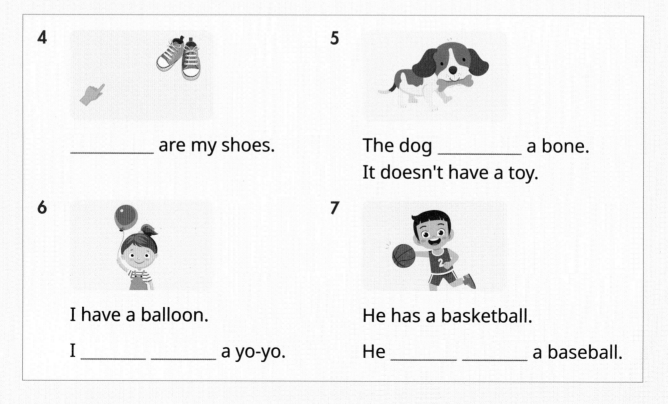

4 _____ are my shoes.

5 The dog _____ a bone.
It doesn't have a toy.

6 I have a balloon.
I _____ _____ a yo-yo.

7 He has a basketball.
He _____ _____ a baseball.

◆ Look and complete the dialogues.

8 _____ this a hippo?

Yes, _____ _____.

9 _____ those gorillas?

No, _____ _____.

10 _____ Ann have an umbrella?

Yes, _____ _____.

11 _____ they have spoons?

No, _____ _____.

◆ Find and correct the mistakes.

e.g. | Those | is | my | backpack.
          a   b   c

(a) → That

12 | These | is | his | boots.
         a   b c

_____ → _____

13 He | don't | have | an eraser.
           a   b

I | have | an eraser.
  c

_____ → _____

14 | This | is | you | T-shirt.
         a   b   c

_____ → _____

I can run.

✦ Listen and circle.

I can run.

I can climb.

But you can't swim.

I can run, climb, swim, and jump!

I can swim.

But you can't jump.

| can | can | can't | can | can't | can |

1 **Can**

Can	
I / You	
He / She / It	**can** run.
We / You / They	
Rabbits	

I **can** run. He **can** jump.

LESSON 2 Can't

Can't	
I / You	
He / She / It	**can't** run.
We / You / They	
Turtles	

can't = cannot

They **can't** run.

We **can't** climb the tree.

A horse **can't** fly.

Rabbits **can't** swim.

Let's Practice

A Look and circle.

1  A kangaroo ⟨can⟩ / can't jump high.

2  Turtles can / can't run.

3  The girl can / can't paint.

B **Look and write *can* or *can't*.**

A monkey ___can___ climb.

The boy ___can't___ climb.

Birds _____ fly.

Goats _____ fly.

The woman _____ ski.

The man _____ ski.

Adam _____ ride a horse.

Kelly _____ ride a horse.

C **Check and write about yourself.**

	swim	ride a bike	speak English	play the violin
I can ...				
I can't ...	✓			

1 _____ I can't swim. _____

2 _____

3 _____

4 _____

✎ **Look and complete the sentences.**

① Ella   can   jump   high.

② Chris   the guitar.

③ The children   .

④ The dog   .

⑤ Sally   the tree.

Modal Verb: Can Questions

Can you walk?

✦ **Listen and circle.**

| can | can | can | can | can | can't |

LESSON

1 Can: How to make a question

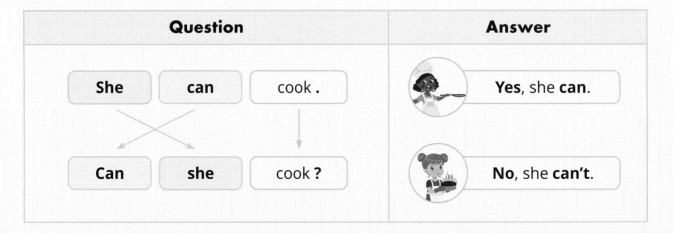

Question			Answer
She	**can**	cook .	**Yes**, she **can**.
Can	**she**	cook ?	**No**, she **can't**.

2 Can: Question and Answer

Question			Answer	
Can	you	**sing**?	**Yes**, I **can**.	**No**, I **can't**.
	he / she / it		**Yes**, he / she / it **can**.	**No**, he / she / it **can't**.
	you / they		**Yes**, we / they **can**.	**No**, we / they **can't**.

Can you cook?
Yes, I **can**.

Can she skate?
Yes, she **can**.

Can it talk?
Yes, it **can**.

Can they ski?
No, they **can't**.

Can they swim?
No, they **can't**.

Let's Practice

 A **Change the sentences to questions.**

1 He can dance. → _____Can_____ _____he_____ dance?

2 Sarah can skate. → _____ _____ skate?

3 Bats can fly. → _____ _____ fly?

B Look and answer the questions.

1 Can the baby walk? _____No_____, he ___can't___.

2 Can Helen ski? _____, she _____.

3 Can parrots talk? _____, they _____.

4 Can you make a cake? _____, I _____.

C Look and write.

_____Can_____ they play tennis?

Yes, ___they___ ___can___.

_____ David climb the tree?

No, _____ _____.

_____ you catch a ball?

Yes, _____ _____.

_____ the dog read?

No, _____ _____.

✎ **Look and complete the dialogues.**

① Q _____Can_____ Robo _____read_____?

A _____Yes_____, he _____can_____.

② Q _____ Rona _____?

A _____, she _____.

③ Q _____ Robo _____?

A _____, he _____.

④ Q _____ Robo and Rona _____?

A _____, they _____.

Review 5

A Look and circle.

	swim	dance	skate	speak English
Amy	O	X	X	O
Luke	X	O	X	O

1 Amy (can) / can't swim.

2 Amy can / can't dance.

3 Luke can / can't swim.

4 Luke can / can't dance.

5 Amy and Luke can / can't skate.

6 Amy and Luke can / can't speak English.

B Look, choose, and write.

①  Hello

②

③

④

talk	ride	jump	ski

1 __Can__ parrots __talk__?
Yes, they can.

2 _____ a rabbit _____?
Yes, it can.

3 _____ she _____?
Yes, she can.

4 _____ he _____ a bike?
No, he can't.

C Look and write.

1

She ___can___ paint.

2

The baby _____ walk.

3

Can turtles run?

No, _____ _____.

4

Can a penguin swim?

Yes, _____ _____.

5

_____ _____ play the violin?

No, I can't.

6

_____ _____ cook?

Yes, he can.

D Correct the mistakes.

1 A monkey <u>cans</u> climbs the tree. → can

2 I <u>cann't</u> ride a horse. →

3 Q Can a parrot talk?

   A Yes, it <u>can't</u>. →

Mini Test 4

• Look and circle.

1  I can / have / has a toy truck.

2 Cats can / can't / doesn't talk.

3  My sister can / can't / has play the violin.

• Look and write.

4

The girl _____ ski.

5

A kangaroo can jump high.

It _____ fly.

6

We have raincoats.

We _____ _____ umbrellas.

7

Andy _____ a scarf.

He doesn't have gloves.

◆ Read and complete the dialogues.

8 Can she dance?

Yes, _____ _____.

9 Does the tree have leaves?

No, _____ _____.

10 _____ _____ have a tent?

Yes, they do.

11 _____ _____ play soccer?

No, I can't.

◆ Find and correct the mistakes.

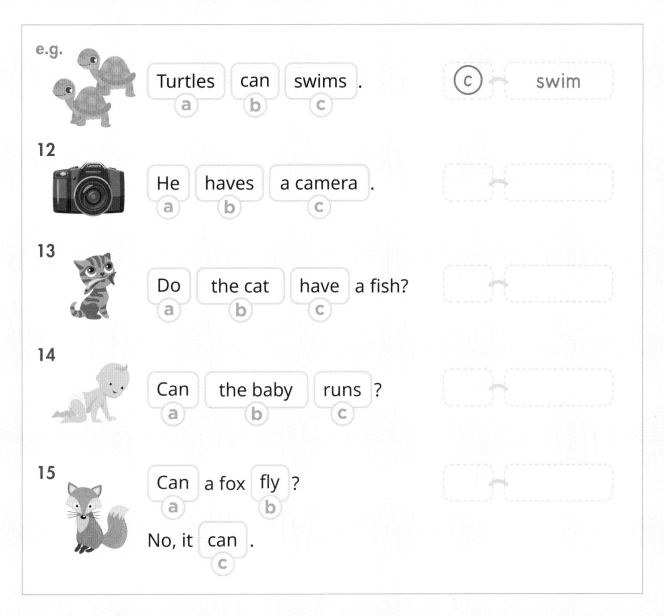

e.g.

| Turtles | can | swims | . |
| a | b | c | |

ⓒ → swim

12

| He | haves | a camera | . |
| a | b | c | |

13

| Do | the cat | have | a fish? |
| a | b | c | |

14

| Can | the baby | runs | ? |
| a | b | c | |

15

| Can | a fox | fly | ? |
| a | | b | |

No, it can .
c

Unit 20

Wh- Question: What and Who

What is it?

✦ **Listen and circle.**

 LESSON

1 What + be ...?

Animals, Things, and Places	
What is it?	**What** are they?
It is **a fish**.	They are **fruits**.
It is **a river**.	They are **baskets**.

82   UNIT 20

2 Who + be ...?

People	
Who is she? She is **my aunt**.	**Who** is he? He is **my uncle**.
Who are you? I am **your teacher**.	**Who** are they? They are **my grandparents**.

Let's Practice

A Read and match.

1 What is it?

2 Who is she?

3 What are they?

4 Who are they?

She is my aunt.

They are my parents.

It is a picture.

They are spiders.

B Look and write the questions.

1

What [is] [it] ?
It is a candle.

2

Who [　　　] [　　　]?
He is my brother.

3

What [　　　] [　　　] ?
They are rulers.

4

Who [　　　] [　　　]?
They are my grandparents.

C Look and write.

1

_____Who_____ are they?
_____They_____ _____are_____ my cousins.

2

_____ is it?
_____ _____ a diary.

3

_____ are they?
_____ _____ pandas.

4

_____ is she?
_____ _____ my aunt.

✏ **Look and complete the questions.**

① Q ___What___ ___is___ ___it___?

A It is a picture.

② Q _____ _____ _____?

A She is my aunt.

③ Q _____ _____ _____?

A It is her camera.

④ Q _____ _____ _____?

A They are my grandparents.

⑤ Q _____ _____ _____?

A They are koalas.

Prepositions of Place

It is under the tree.

✦ **Listen and circle.**

| under | on | in |

 LESSON

1 *on*, *in*, and *under*

on	in	under
on the box	**in** the box	**under** the table

2 Be + *Preposition* + Noun

Where is the duck?
It is **on** the bench.

Where is the chicken?
It is **in** the house.

Where is the cat?
It is **under** the table.

Where are the dogs?
They are **under** the tree.

Where are the bees?
They are **on** the flowers.

Let's Practice

A Look and find the correct pictures.

a

b

c

d

1 It's on the chair. 　d　

2 They're in the box. ☐

3 They're on the box. ☐

4 It's under the chair. ☐

B Look, circle, and write.

①   ②   ③   ④

1 (under) / on   The ball is _____under_____ the desk.

2   in / on   The bees are _____ the flower.

3   in / under   The cats are _____ the basket.

4   under / on   The dog is _____ the table.

C Choose and write with *in*, *on*, or *under*.

bowl   basket   box   cheese

1

Where is the fish?

It's ____in____ the ___bowl___.

2

Where is the mouse?

It's _____ the _____.

3

Where are the apples?

They're _____ the _____.

4

Where are the birds?

They're _____ the _____.

Let's Write

Where are the toys? Look at the two pictures and write.

① Picture A The doll is ___on___ the ___chair___ .

Picture B The doll is _____ the ___box___ .

② Picture A The balls are _____ the ___table___ .

Picture B The balls are _____ the _____ .

③ Picture A The rocket is _____ the _____ .

Picture B The rocket is _____ the _____ .

A Look and match.

1 Where is the ball?

They are on the box.

2 Who is he?

They are pandas.

3 What are they?

He is my brother.

4 Where are the balls?

It is in the box.

B Look, circle, and write.

① 　② 　③ 　④

1 They are ____on____ the flower.

in / (on)

2 It is _____ the chair.

under / on

3 They are _____ the basket.

in / under

4 It is _____ the leaf.

in / on

C Read, circle, and write.

1   Who / (What) is it?

    ___It___ ___is___ an album.

2   Who / What are they?

    _____ _____ my parents.

3   Who / What are they?

    _____ _____ ducks.

4   Who / What is he?

    _____ _____ my uncle.

D Look and write.

1

___Who___ ___are___ ___they___ ?

They are my grandparents.

2

_____ _____ _____?

It is a candle.

3

_____ _____ _____?

She is my aunt.

4

Where is the mouse?

It is _____ the cheese.

5

Where is the fish?

It is _____ the bowl.

6

Where is the bird?

It is _____ the box.

Mini Test 5

◆ **Look and check.**

1   ☐ What is it?
      ☐ What are they?

2   ☐ Can the girl swim?
      ☐ Can the girl swims?

3   ☐ Who is it?
      ☐ What is it?

◆ **Look and write.**

4 It's _____ the bench.

5 A parrot _____ talk.

6 It's _____ the house.

7 She _____ skate.

8 They _____ ski.

9 It's _____ the table.

Read and complete the dialogues.

10 _____ is he?

_____ _____ my uncle.

11 _____ _____ speak English?

No, they can't.

12 _____ are they?

_____ _____ fruits.

13 Can a monkey climb the tree?

Yes, _____ _____.

Find and correct the mistakes.

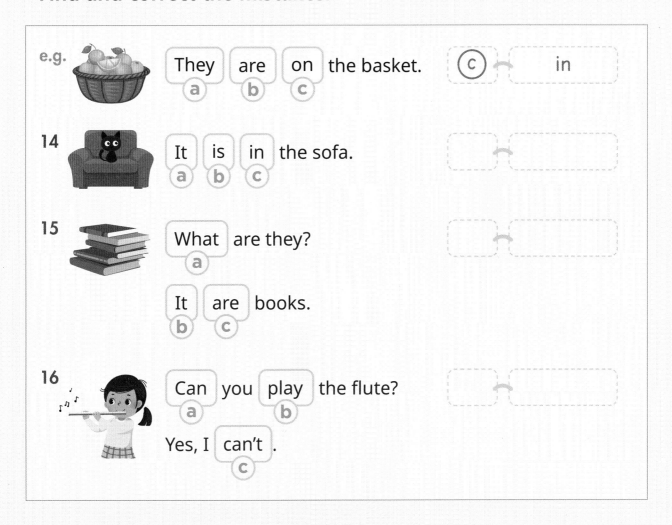

e.g.

They are on the basket.
a   b   c

c → in

14 It is in the sofa.
a b c

15 What are they?
a

It are books.
b c

16 Can you play the flute?
a   b

Yes, I can't.
c

Grammar Audio Lessons

- If you need help to understand the grammar, scan the QR code using your phone.
- This will give you immediate access to detailed audio lessons in Korean.
- You can select and play each lesson from the list.

Unit 01
1. Nouns
2. a/an + Noun

Unit 02
1. Noun + s
2. Noun + es

Unit 03
1. Places, Animals, and Things
2. People

Unit 05
1. Pronoun + Be
2. Short forms

Unit 06
1. Pronoun + Be + Not
2. Short forms

Unit 07
1. Be Verb: How to make a question
2. Be Verb: Question and Answer

Unit 09
1. This vs. That / These vs. Those
2. This / That
3. These / Those

Unit 10
1. Questions: This / That
2. Questions: These / Those

Unit 11	① My / Your / Our	② His / Her / Its / Their
Unit 13	① Have	② Has
Unit 14	① Don't Have	② Doesn't Have
Unit 15	① Do you have …?	② Do we/they have …?
	③ Does he/she/it have …?	
Unit 17	① Can	② Can't
Unit 18	① Can: How to make a question	② Can: Question and Answer
Unit 20	① What + be …?	② Who + be …?
Unit 21	① on, in, and under	② Be + Preposition + Noun

Scope & Sequence

Unit	Grammar Point	Key Sentences	Key Vocabulary
01	**Nouns and Articles (a/an)**	It is a banana. It is an apple.	a zoo, a banana, a girl, a monkey, an apple, an elephant, an igloo, an orange, an umbrella
02	**Plural Noun:** -s, -es	They are books. They are dishes.	books, chairs, watches, dishes, buses, boxes
03	**Subject Pronoun:** I, we, you, he, she, it, they	I am Danny. He is my father. She is my mother.	house, dog, tree, father, mother, sister, friend, family
04	**Review 1**		
05	**Be Verb: Positives**	I am a teacher. You are a student. He is a bus driver.	school, teacher, student, bus driver, bus
06	**Be Verb: Negatives**	I am not sad. She is not excited. They are not full.	sad, happy, sleepy, angry, excited, hungry, full, big, small
07	**Be Verb: Questions**	Are you a doctor? Is he a cook? Is she a firefighter?	cook, baker, doctor, nurse, firefighter, teacher, pilot, scientist
08	**Review 2 + Mini Test 1** (Unit 01-07)		
09	**Demonstrative Pronoun:** this, that, these, those	This is a lion. That is a tiger. These aren't lions. Those are lions.	lion, tiger, gorilla, monkey, panda, bear, bee, ant, bat, bird
10	**Demonstrative Pronoun:** this, that, these, those Questions	Is this a cat? Is that a dog? Are those rabbits?	dog, cat, snake, iguana, hamster, rabbit, pig
11	**Possessive Adjective:** my, our, your, his, her, its, their	This is his T-shirt. That is her dress. These are their bags.	T-shirt, dress, hat, socks, book, bag, toy
12	**Review 3 + Mini Test 2** (Unit 05-11)		

Unit	Grammar Point	Key Sentences	Key Vocabulary
13	**Present Simple: Positives**	I have a robot. He has a toy car. They have balloons.	toy car, doll, robot, ball, yo-yo, balloon
14	**Present Simple: Negatives**	I don't have a camera. She doesn't have a map. They don't have raincoats.	camera, map, raincoat, glove, umbrella, pen, fork
15	**Present Simple: Questions**	Do you have a bat? Does he have a basketball? Do they have skateboards?	baseball, bat, basketball, jump rope, skateboard, bike
16	**Review 4 + Mini Test 3** (Unit 09-15)		
17	**Modal Verb:** Can, Can't	I can run. He can jump. We can't climb the tree.	run, climb, swim, jump, fly
18	**Modal Verb:** Can Questions	Can you cook? Can she skate? Can they swim?	walk, talk, eat, cook, skate, ski, swim
19	**Review 5 + Mini Test 4** (Unit 13-18)		
20	**Wh- Question:** What, Who	What is it? What are they? Who is she?	picture, fruit, basket, fish, river, aunt, uncle, cousin, grandparent
21	**Prepositions of Place:** on, in, under	It is on the bench. It is in the house. They are under the tree.	tree, flower, rock, bench, table, house, box
22	**Review 6 + Mini Test 5** (Unit 17-21)		

Spiral Syllabus

Oh! My Grammar 1

U01	Nouns and Articles (a/an)
U02	Plural Nouns
U03	Subject Pronouns
U04	Review 1
U05	Be Verb: Positives
U06	Be Verb: Negatives
U07	Be Verb: Questions
U08	Review 2
U09	Demonstrative Pronouns
U10	Demonstrative Pronoun: Questions
U11	Possessive Adjectives
U12	Review 3
U13	Present Simple: Positives
U14	Present Simple: Negatives
U15	Present Simple: Questions
U16	Review 4
U17	Modal Verb: Can/Can't
U18	Modal Verb: Can Questions
U19	Review 5
U20	Wh- Question: What and Who
U21	Prepositions of Place
U22	Review 6

Oh! My Grammar 2

U01	Nouns and Articles (a/an/the)
U02	Plural Nouns
U03	Count and Non-count Nouns
U04	Demonstratives and Possessives
U05	Review 1
U06	Be Verb: Positives and Negatives
U07	Be Verb: Questions
U08	There + Be + Noun
U09	Adjectives
U10	Review 2
U11	Present Simple: Positives
U12	Present Simple: Negatives
U13	Present Simple: Questions
U14	Review 3
U15	Present Continuous: Positives
U16	Present Continuous: Negatives
U17	Present Continuous: Questions
U18	Review 4
U19	Modal Verb: Can / May
U20	Wh- Question: What, Who, and Whose
U21	Prepositions of Time
U22	Review 5

Oh! My Grammar 3

U01	Nouns and Articles (a/an/the)
U02	Present Simple: Be Verbs
U03	There + Be + Noun
U04	Review 1
U05	Present Simple: Positives and Negatives
U06	Present Simple: Questions
U07	Present Continuous: Positives and Negatives
U08	Present Continuous: Questions
U09	Review 2
U10	Let's and Imperatives
U11	Future: Positives and Negatives
U12	Future: Questions
U13	Review 3
U14	Past: Be Verbs
U15	Past: Regular Verbs
U16	Past: Irregular Verbs
U17	Past: Questions
U18	Review 4
U19	Wh- Question: What, Who, Whose, Where, and When
U20	Adjectives and Adverbs
U21	Comparatives
U22	Review 5

1 구문 판매 1위 '천일문' 콘텐츠를 활용하여 정확하고 다양한 구문 학습

끊어읽기 해석하기 문장 구조 분석 해설·해석 제공 단어 스크램블링 영작하기

2 문법·서술형 쎄듀의 모든 문법 문항을 활용하여 내신까지 해결하는 정교한 문법 유형 제공

객관식과 주관식의 결합 문법 포인트별 학습 보기를 활용한 집합 문항 내신대비 서술형 어법+서술형 문제

3 어휘 초·중·고·공무원까지 방대한 어휘량을 제공하며 오프라인 TEST 인쇄도 가능

영단어 카드 학습 단어 ↔ 뜻 유형 예문 활용 유형 단어 매칭 게임

4 선생님 보유 문항 이용

Online Test OMR Test

with 세이펜

원어민 발음을 실시간 반복학습	단어 및 예문의 우리말 해석 듣기	혼자서도 쉽게 정답 확인 가능

세이펜 핀파일 다운로드 안내

STEP ① 세이펜과 컴퓨터를 USB 케이블로 연결하세요.

STEP ② 쎄듀북 홈페이지(www.cedubook.com)에 접속 후, 학습자료실 메뉴에서 학습할 교재를 찾아 이동합니다.

> 초등교재 ▶ ELT ▶ 학습교재 클릭 ▶ 세이펜 핀파일 자료 클릭
> ▶ 다운로드 (저장을 '다른 이름으로 저장'으로 변경하여 저장소를 USB로 변경) ▶ 완료

STEP ③ 음원 다운로드가 완료되면 세이펜과 컴퓨터의 USB 케이블을 분리하세요.

STEP ④ 세이펜을 분리하면 "시스템을 초기화 중입니다. 잠시만 기다려 주세요."라는 멘트가 나옵니다.

STEP ⑤ 멘트 종료 후 세이펜을 〈Oh! My Grammar〉 표지에 대보세요.
효과음이 나온 후 바로 학습을 시작할 수 있습니다.

참고사항

◆ 세이펜은 본 교재에 포함되어 있지 않습니다. 별도로 구매하여 이용할 수 있으며, 기존에 보유하신 세이펜이 있다면 핀파일만 다운로드해서
  바로 이용하실 수 있습니다.

◆ 세이펜에서 제작된 모든 기종(기존에 보유하고 계신 기종도 호환 가능)으로 사용이 가능합니다.

◆ 모든 기종은 세이펜에서 권장하는 최신 펌웨어 업데이트를 진행해 주시기 바랍니다.
  업데이트는 세이펜 홈페이지(www.saypen.com)에서 가능합니다.

◆ 핀파일은 쎄듀북 홈페이지(www.cedubook.com)와 세이펜 홈페이지(www.saypen.com)에서 모두 다운로드 가능합니다.

◆ 세이펜을 이용하지 않는 학습자는 쎄듀북 홈페이지 부가학습자료, 교재 내 QR코드 이미지 등을 활용하여 원어민 음성으로 학습하실 수 있습니다.

◆ 기타 문의사항은 www.cedubook.com / 02-3272-4766으로 연락 바랍니다.

Oh! My Grammar

1

Workbook

CEDU BOOK

Oh! My Grammar 1

Workbook

CEDU BOOK

Contents

Nouns & Pronouns

Be Verbs

Demonstratives & Possessives

Present Simple

Modal Verb *can*

Wh- Questions & Prepositions

Unit 01

It is a banana.

Step 1 Choose and write in the correct box.

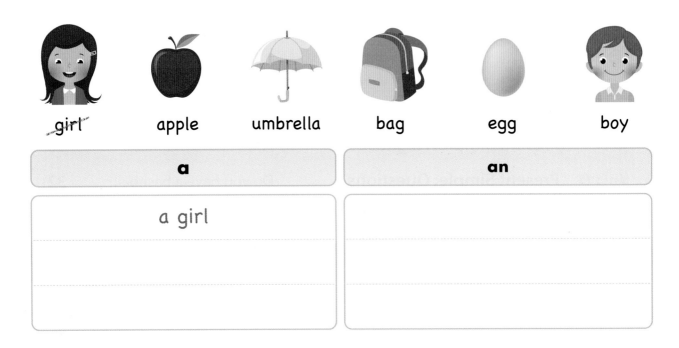

girl   apple   umbrella   bag   egg   boy

a	an
a girl	

Step 2 Look, choose, and write.

watch   zoo   banana   elephant   hat   octopus

1

It is ____a watch____.

2

It is _____.

3

It is _____.

4

It is _____.

5

It is _____.

6

It is _____.

Unscramble and write the sentences.

1 | mouse | a | . | It is |

→ It is a mouse.

2 | It is | ant | an | . |

→ _____

3 | orange | . | It is | an |

→ _____

4 | a | . | school | It is |

→ _____

5 | igloo | It is | an | . |

→ _____

6 | . | monkey | a | It is |

→ _____

Unit 02 They are books.

Step 1 Choose and write in the correct box.

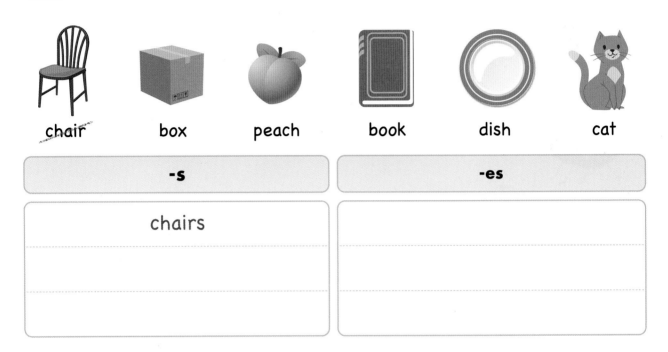

chair   box   peach   book   dish   cat

-s	-es
chairs	

Step 2 Look, choose, and write.

watch   egg   bus   dish   ant   banana

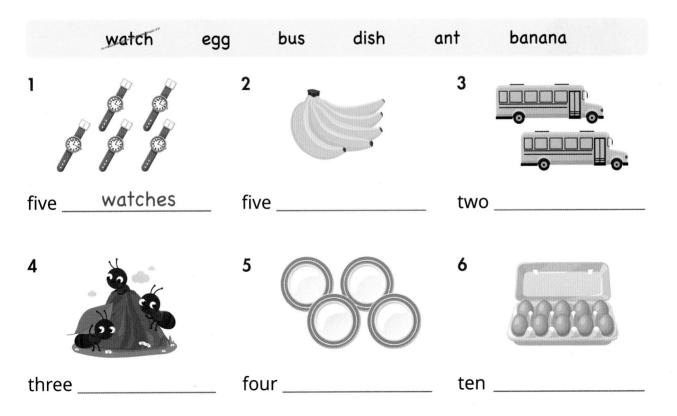

1 five ___watches___

2 five _____

3 two _____

4 three _____

5 four _____

6 ten _____

Look and match. Then, write the sentences.

1

They are

book   -s .

box   -es .

→ They are boxes.

2

They are

dish   -s .

pen   -es .

→ _____

3

They are

sock   -s .

watch   -es .

→ _____

4

They are

bench   -s .

table   -es .

→ _____

5

They are

pencil   -s .

brush   -es .

→ _____

Unit 03   I am Danny.

Step 1 **Look, circle, and write.**

1

(I)
You

_____I_____ am a student.

2

It
They

_____ is a bus.

3

She
He

_____ is my teacher.

4

He
They

_____ are my brothers.

Step 2 **Look, choose, and write.**

we   you   he   I   she   they

1

__We__ are friends.

2

_____ am Kate.

3

_____ are my sister.

4

_____ is my dad.

5

_____ is my mom.

6

_____ are my family.

Unscramble and write the sentences.

1

She | my sister | is | .

→ She is my sister.

2

my brother | is | . | He

→ _____

3

my mother | . | She | is

→ _____

4

are | . | dogs | They

→ _____

5

a ring | It | is | .

→ _____

6

You | my friend | . | are

→ _____

Review 1

Step 1 ▶ **Look, circle, and write.**

1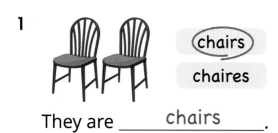

(chairs)

chaires

They are ___chairs___.

2

a egg

an egg

It is _____.

3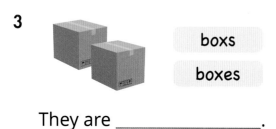

boxs

boxes

They are _____.

4

a wolf

an wolf

It is _____.

Step 2 ▶ **Look, choose, and write.**

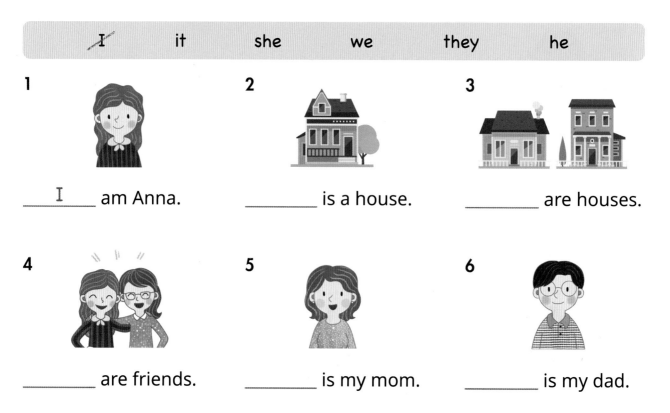

| ~~I~~ | it | she | we | they | he |

1 ___I___ am Anna.

2 _____ is a house.

3 _____ are houses.

4 _____ are friends.

5 _____ is my mom.

6 _____ is my dad.

Step 3 Correct the mistakes. Then, write the sentences.

1  It is <u>an</u> banana.

→ It is a banana.

2 They are <u>lamp</u>.

→ _____

3 <u>They</u> is my horse.

→ _____

4  It is <u>a</u> orange.

→ _____

5  They are <u>benchs</u>.

→ _____

6 He are my brothers.

→ _____

Unit 05 He is a bus driver.

Step 1 Look, match, and write.

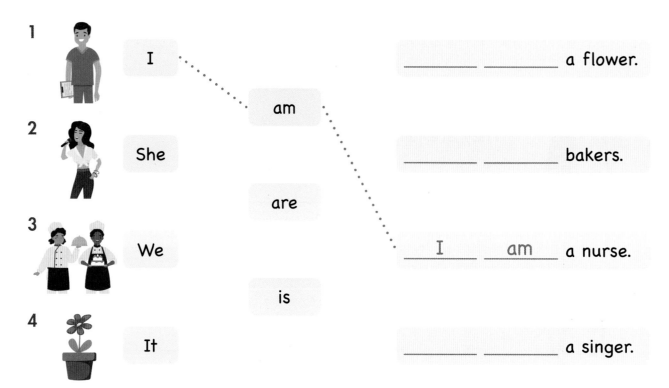

1 I

2 She

3 We

4 It

am

are

is

_____ _____ a flower.

_____ _____ bakers.

___I___ ___am___ a nurse.

_____ _____ a singer.

Step 2 Look and write.

① He ② You ③ It ④ I

1 ___He___ ___is___ a bus driver. = ___He's___ a bus driver.

2 _____ _____ a student. = _____ a student.

3 _____ _____ a bus. = _____ a bus.

4 _____ _____ a teacher. = _____ a teacher.

Look and circle. Then, write the sentences.

1  She / (He)   am / are / (is)   a cook.

→ He is a cook.

2  I / We   am / are / is   firefighters.

→ _____

3  I / We   am / are / is   a student.

→ _____

4  It / They   am / are / is   crayons.

→ _____

5  She / He   am / are / is   a dancer.

→ _____

6  It / They   am / are / is   a map.

→ _____

They are not full.

Step 1 Read, check, and write.

1 They ___are not___ hungry. ☐ is not ☑ are not

2 I _____ a nurse. ☐ am not ☐ are not

3 We _____ sleepy. ☐ is not ☐ are not

4 He _____ angry. ☐ is not ☐ are not

5 It _____ a cat. ☐ am not ☐ is not

6 You _____ excited. ☐ is not ☐ are not

Step 2 Look and write.

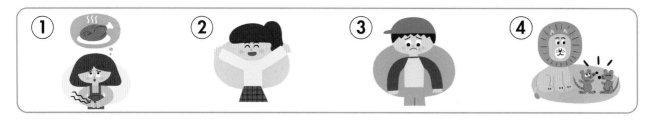

1 She is hungry. She ___isn't___ full.

2 I am happy. _____ _____ angry.

3 He is sad. He _____ happy.

4 They are small. They _____ big.

Unscramble and write the sentences.

1

okay   is   .   She   not

→ She is not okay.

2

We   cold   not   .   are

→ _____

3

happy   You   aren't   .

→ _____

4

not   .   long   is   It

→ _____

5

a teacher   .   not   I'm

→ _____

6

He   a doctor   isn't   .

→ _____

Unit 07 Is he a cook?

Step 1 Read, write, and match.

1 ___Is___ she a doctor? .... Yes, I am.

2 _____ they pilots? .... Yes, she is.

3 _____ you a student? .... No, it isn't.

4 _____ it an elephant? .... No, they aren't.

Step 2 Look and complete the dialogues.

1

__Is__ she a cook?

Yes, __she__ __is__ .

2

_____ they teachers?

No, _____ _____ .

3

_____ you a doctor?

Yes, _____ _____ .

4

_____ it a duck?

No, _____ _____ .

1

Q <u>Are you a bus driver?</u>

a bus driver / Are / you / ?

A No, I'm not.

2

Q _____

? / they / horses / Are

A Yes, they are.

3

Q _____

? / Is / a pilot / she

A No, she isn't.

4

Q _____

Is / a nurse / ? / he

A Yes, he is.

5

Q _____

firefighters / ? / Are / they

A Yes, they are.

6

Q _____

a butterfly / ? / Is / it

A No, it isn't.

Review 2

Step 1 **Read, circle, and write.**

1 She ____is____ a scientist.

(is) are

2 I _____ a police officer.

am are

3 They _____ bakers.

isn't aren't

4 The elephant _____ small.

isn't aren't

5 We _____ sleepy.

is are

6 The baby _____ hungry.

isn't aren't

Step 2 **Look and write.**

1

He ___is___ a student.
He __isn't__ a teacher.

2

We _____ bakers.
We _____ pilots.

3

It _____ a cow.
It _____ a horse.

4

_____ you a cook?
No, _____ _____.

5

_____ she sick?
Yes, _____ _____.

6

_____ they pencils?
No, _____ _____.

Unscramble and write the sentences.

1.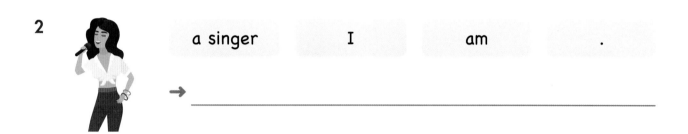

   are   horses   .   They

   → They are horses.

2.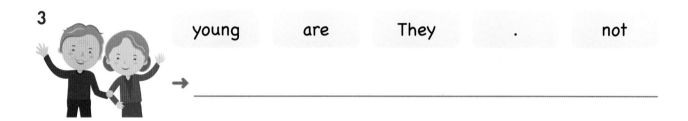

   a singer   I   am   .

   →

3.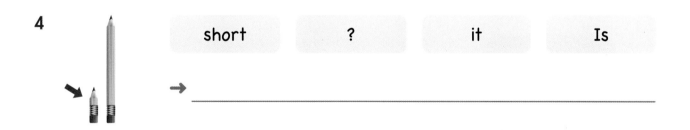

   young   are   They   .   not

   →

4.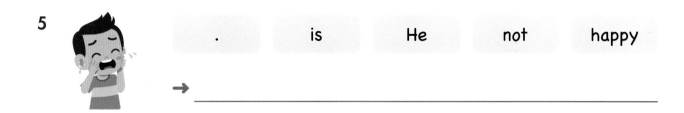

   short   ?   it   Is

   →

5.

   .   is   He   not   happy

   →

Unit 09 This is a lion.

Step 1 Look and write *this*, *that*, *these*, or *those*.

1

_____This_____ is a zebra.

2

_____ is a lion.

3

_____ are ants.

4

_____ are apples.

Step 2 Look, circle, and write.

1

This / (That) _____isn't_____ a cow.

2

This / That _____ a pencil.

3

That / Those _____ tigers.

4

This / These _____ bats.

Circle and write the sentences.

1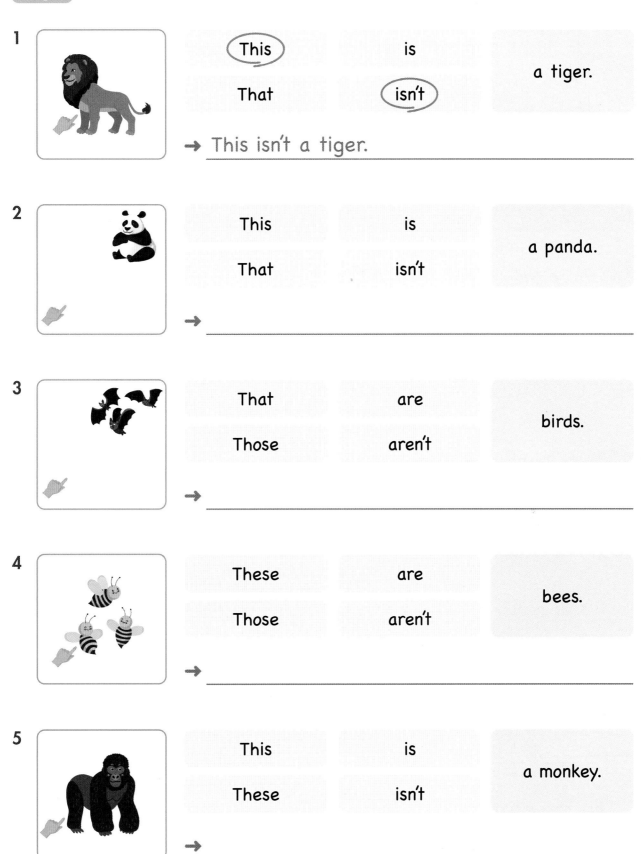

This   is

That   isn't

a tiger.

→ This isn't a tiger.

2

This   is

That   isn't

a panda.

→ _____

3

That   are

Those   aren't

birds.

→ _____

4

These   are

Those   aren't

bees.

→ _____

5

This   is

These   isn't

a monkey.

→ _____

Unit 10 Is this a cat?

Step 1 Look and write with *this*, *that*, *these*, or *those*.

①  ②  ③  ④

1 ___Are___ ___these___ bees?   Yes, they are.

2 _____ _____ a chicken?   No, it isn't.

3 _____ _____ a rabbit?   Yes, it is.

4 _____ _____ dogs?   No, they aren't.

Step 2 Look and complete the dialogues.

1

Is this a cat?

No, ___it___ ___isn't___ .

2

Is that a cat?

Yes, _____ _____ .

3

Are these hamsters?

No, _____ _____ .

4

Are those pigs?

Yes, _____ _____ .

Unscramble and write the questions.

1

Q <u>Is that a horse?</u>

a horse / that / Is / ?

A No, it isn't. It's a cow.

2

Q _____

turtles / ? / Are / these

A Yes, they are.

3

Q _____

? / this / a snake / Is

A No, it isn't. It's an iguana.

4

Q _____

these / Are / ? / hamsters

A Yes, they are.

5

Q _____

a monkey / that / Is / ?

A Yes, it is.

6

Q _____

lions / Are / ? / those

A No, they aren't. They are elephants.

Unit 11 This is his T-shirt.

Step 1 Look, match, and write.

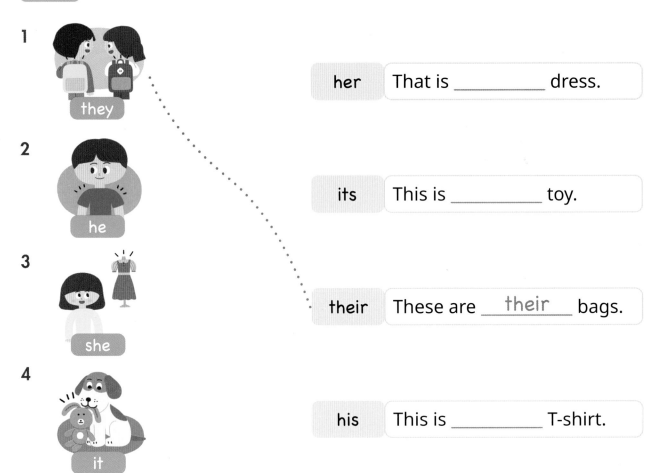

1 they

her | That is _____ dress.

2 he

its | This is _____ toy.

3 she

their | These are ___their___ bags.

4 it

his | This is _____ T-shirt.

Step 2 Look and write.

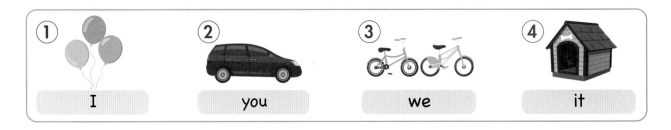

① I ② you ③ we ④ it

1 These are ____my____ balloons.

2 This is _____ car.

3 These are _____ bicycles.

4 This is _____ house.

Unscramble and write the sentences.

1.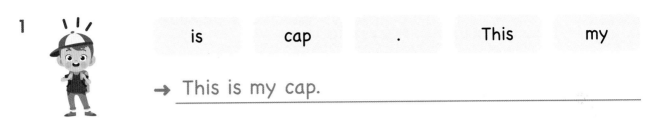
   is   cap   .   This   my

   → This is my cap.

2.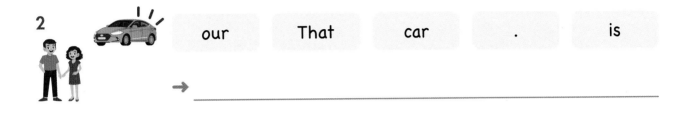
   our   That   car   .   is

   → _____

3.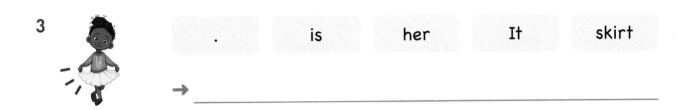
   .   is   her   It   skirt

   → _____

4.
   are   bikes   .   their   These

   → _____

5.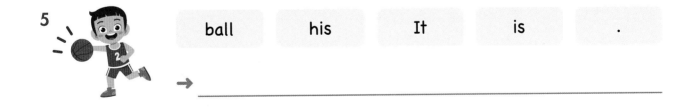
   ball   his   It   is   .

   → _____

6.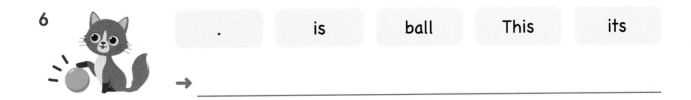
   .   is   ball   This   its

   → _____

Review 3

Step 1 ▸ Look, choose, and write.

her	its	their	his

1 That is _____her_____ dress.

2 This is _____ dog.

3 This is _____ toy.

4 Those are _____ toys.

Step 2 ▸ Look and write.

1

_____Those_____ are hamsters.

2

_____ is a bag.

3

_____ aren't pandas.

4

_____ isn't a cat.

5

_____ this a balloon?

No, _____ _____ .

6

_____ those birds?

Yes, _____ _____ .

Circle and write the sentences.

1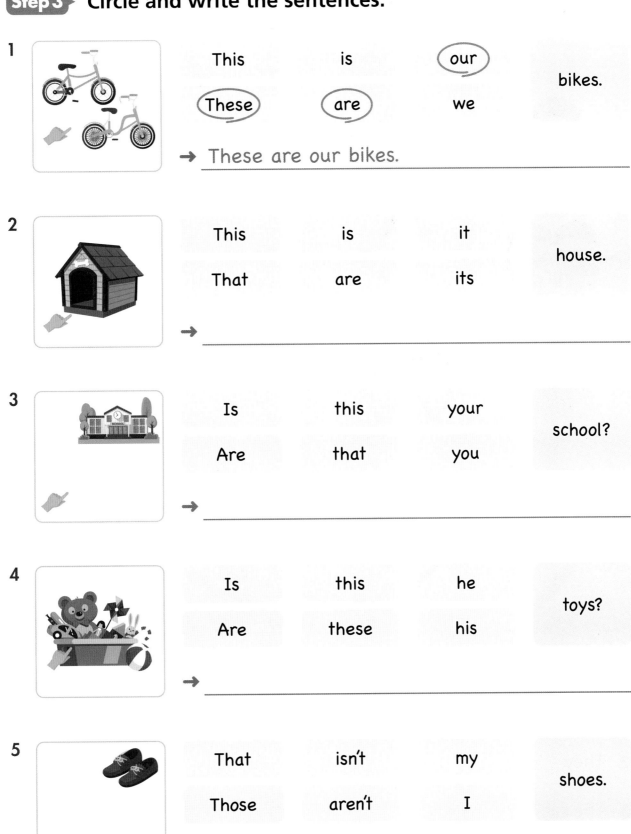

This	is	(our)
(These)	(are)	we

bikes.

→ These are our bikes.

2

This	is	it
That	are	its

house.

→ _____

3

Is	this	your
Are	that	you

school?

→ _____

4

Is	this	he
Are	these	his

toys?

→ _____

5

That	isn't	my
Those	aren't	I

shoes.

→ _____

Unit 13 We have dolls.

Step 1 Look and write *have* or *has*.

1 I ____have____ a robot.

2 She _____ a doll.

3 We _____ robots.

4 Mark _____ a toy car.

5 The dog _____ a ball.

6 The girls _____ dolls.

Step 2 Choose and write with *have* or *has*.

a pencil   crayons   balloons   a box

1 He ____has____ ____a____ ____pencil____.

2 They _____ _____.

3 The cat _____ _____ _____.

4 Tom and Bella _____ _____.

Unscramble and write the sentences.

1

a kite   .   has   She

→ She has a kite.

2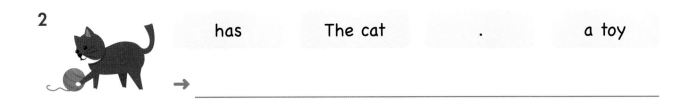

has   The cat   .   a toy

→ _____

3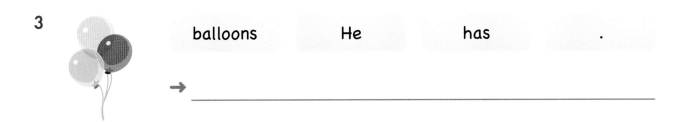

balloons   He   has   .

→ _____

4

The students   .   notebooks   have

→ _____

5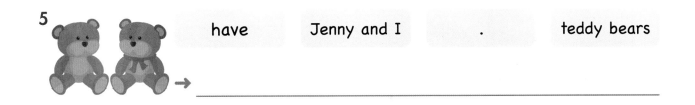

have   Jenny and I   .   teddy bears

→ _____

Unit 14   I don't have a camera.

Step 1   **What's missing? Look, circle, and write.**

1 You _____don't have_____ a tent.   (don't have) / doesn't have

2 Susan _____ gloves.   don't have / doesn't have

3 He _____ a scarf.   don't have / doesn't have

4 Tom and I _____ a map.   don't have / doesn't have

Step 2   **Look and write _have_, _has_, _don't have_, or _doesn't have_.**

1

Frogs _____have_____ legs.

Snakes _____ legs.

2

A horse _____ a tail.

A gorilla _____ a tail.

3

Chickens _____ wings.

Cats _____ wings.

Unscramble and write the sentences.

1

| doesn't | . | gloves | have | She |

→ She doesn't have gloves.

2

| wings | A fox | doesn't | . | have |

→ _____

3

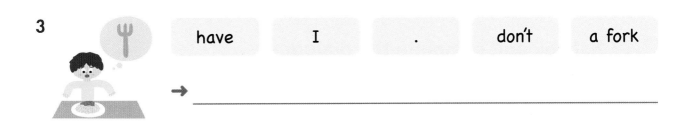

| have | I | . | don't | a fork |

→ _____

4

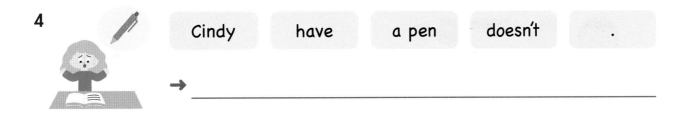

| Cindy | have | a pen | doesn't | . |

→ _____

5

| . | don't | have | They | an umbrella |

→ _____

Unit 15 Do you have a baseball?

Step 1 **Look, circle, and write.**

①  ②  ③  ④

1 (Do) / Does you have bikes? ___Yes___, we ___do___.

2 Do / Does they have a soccer ball? _____, they _____.

3 Do / Does Mike have a skateboard? _____, he _____.

4 Do / Does the mouse have cheese? _____, it _____.

Step 2 **Look and complete the dialogues.**

1   ___Does___ ___she___ have a bat?
Yes, she does.

2   _____ _____ have skates?
No, we don't.

3   _____ the cat have a ball?
No, _____ _____.

4   _____ they have a jump rope?
Yes, _____ _____.

Step 3 **Unscramble and write the questions.**

1

have Do skis ? they

Q Do they have skis?

A Yes, they do.

2

? have the boy Does a baseball

Q _____

A Yes, he does.

3

a bike you have ? Do

Q _____

A No, I don't.

4

have Does a frog wings ?

Q _____

A No, it doesn't.

5

? helmets Do you have

Q _____

A Yes, we do.

Step 1 **Read, circle, and write.**

1   have / (has)   Chloe ____has____ a notebook.

2   don't have / doesn't have   I _____ _____ a brother.

3   have / has   Chickens _____ wings.

4   don't have / doesn't have   He _____ _____ a camera.

5   have / has   The dog _____ a bone.

Step 2 **Look and write.**

I

Kevin

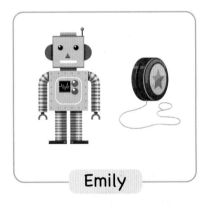
Emily

1 I ____have____ a teddy bear.

2 Kevin _____ a toy car.

3 Emily _____ _____ a baseball.

4 Emily and I _____ _____ a bat.

5 _____ Kevin have a robot?   No, _____ _____.

6 _____ you and Emily have yo-yos?   Yes, _____ _____.

Unscramble and write the sentences.

1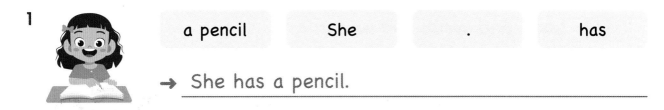

| a pencil | She | . | has |

→ She has a pencil.

2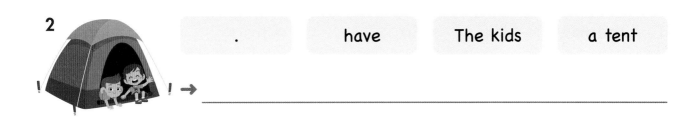

| . | have | The kids | a tent |

→ _____

3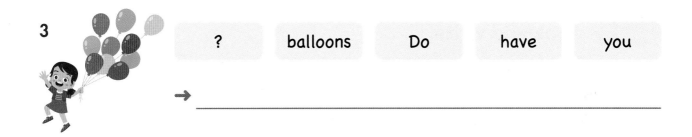

| ? | balloons | Do | have | you |

→ _____

4

| he | ? | have | a skateboard | Does |

→ _____

5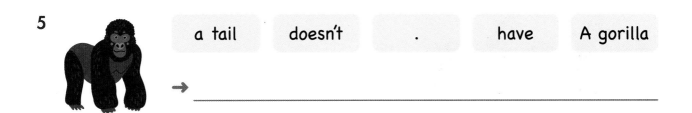

| a tail | doesn't | . | have | A gorilla |

→ _____

Unit 17 I can run.

Step 1 **Look and write *can* or *can't*.**

1 A monkey ____can't____ swim.

2 A frog _____ jump.

3 He _____ play the violin.

4 Penguins _____ fly.

Step 2 **Look and write.**

1

ski

The girl ____can____ ____ski____.

The boy _____ _____.

2

fly

Birds _____ _____.

Goats _____ _____.

3

ride

Leo _____ _____ a horse.

Amy _____ _____ a horse.

Look and write.

	speak English	play tennis	climb a tree
Tom	O	X	O
Anna	X	O	O

1 Tom _____ can _____ speak _____ English.

2 Anna _____ _____ English.

3 Tom _____ _____ tennis.

4 Tom and Anna _____ _____ a tree.

	ride a bike	play the piano	fly a kite
Ben	X	O	X
Cindy	O	O	X

5 Ben _____ _____ a bike.

6 Ben _____ _____ the piano.

7 Cindy _____ _____ the piano.

8 Ben and Cindy _____ _____ a kite.

Modal Verb: Can Questions

Can you walk?

Step 1 Look, write, and match.

① Hello   talk

② cook

③ ride

④ run

1 ___Can___ they ___talk___ ? ....   No, he can't.

2 _____ she _____ ?   Yes, they can.

3 _____ you _____ a bike?   Yes, she can.

4 _____ the baby _____ ?   No, I can't.

Step 2 Look and complete the dialogues.

1

___Can___ you skate?

Yes, ___we___ ___can___ .

2

_____ he climb the tree?

No, _____ _____ .

3

_____ she make a cake?

Yes, _____ _____ .

4

_____ the penguins fly?

No, _____ _____ .

Unscramble and write the questions.

1

?   Anna   skate   Can

Q Can Anna skate?

A Yes, she can.

2

cook   Can   ?   the boy

Q _____

A Yes, he can.

3

the birds   swim   ?   Can

Q _____

A No, they can't.

4

Hello

Can   talk   the parrot   ?

Q _____

A Yes, it can.

5

ski   Can   ?   the children

Q _____

A No, they can't.

Step 1 **Look and write.**

1
sing

It __can__ __sing__ .

2
play

Leo _____ _____ the violin.

3
run

_____ he _____?
No, he can't.

4
cook

_____ you _____?
Yes, I can.

Step 2 **Look and write.**

	play the guitar	catch a ball	ride a bike	swim
Kate	O	O	X	X
Noah	X	O	O	X

1 Kate ____can____ ____play____ the guitar.

2 Noah _____ _____ the guitar.

3 Kate and Noah _____ _____ a ball.

4 Can Noah ride a bike? _____, _____ _____.

5 Can Kate and Noah swim? _____, _____ _____.

Unscramble and write the sentences.

1
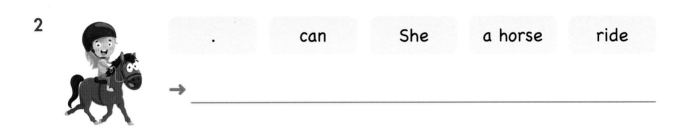

| can | . | skate | The children |

→ The children can skate.

2
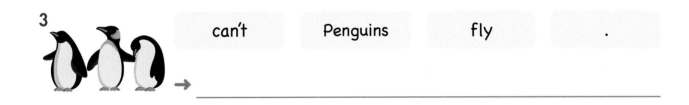

| . | can | She | a horse | ride |

→ _____

3
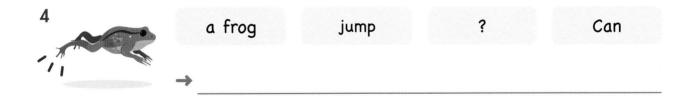

| can't | Penguins | fly | . |

→ _____

4
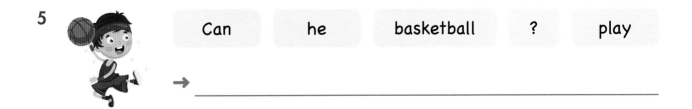

| a frog | jump | ? | Can |

→ _____

5

| Can | he | basketball | ? | play |

→ _____

Unit 20 What is it?

Step 1 Circle and write the questions.

1 (What) / Who ____is____ ____it____ ?   It is an eraser.

2 What / Who _____ _____ ?   I am Sam's sister.

3 What / Who _____ _____ ?   They are kangaroos.

4 What / Who _____ _____ ?   She is my grandma.

5 What / Who _____ _____ ?   They are my friends.

6 What / Who _____ _____ ?   It is a picture.

Step 2 Look and complete the dialogues.

1

____What____ is it?

____It____ ____is____ a camera.

2

_____ is he?

_____ _____ my brother.

3

_____ are they?

_____ _____ rulers.

4

_____ are they?

_____ _____ my parents.

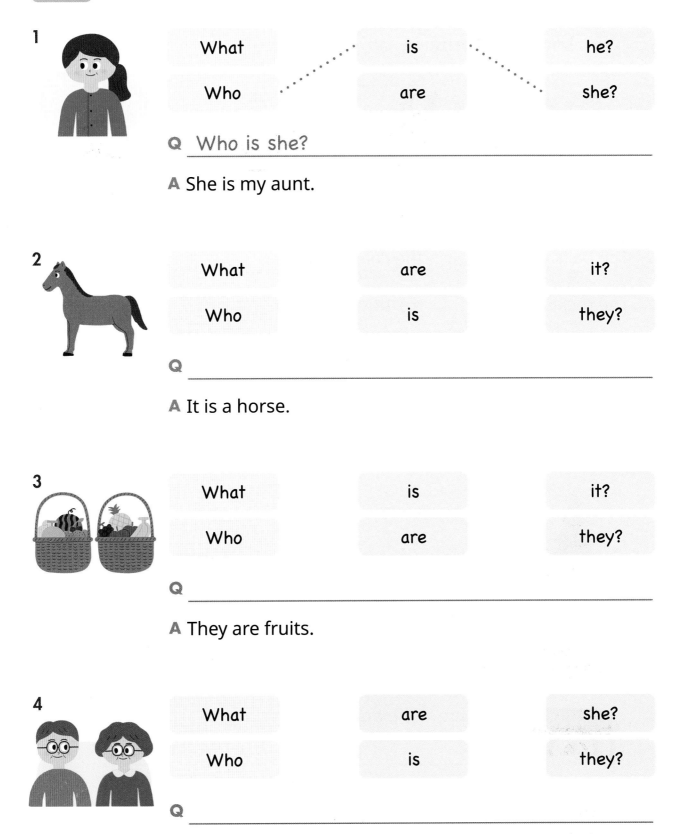

Step 3 **Look, match, and write.**

1

| What | is | he? |
| Who | are | she? |

Q Who is she?

A She is my aunt.

2

| What | are | it? |
| Who | is | they? |

Q _____

A It is a horse.

3

| What | is | it? |
| Who | are | they? |

Q _____

A They are fruits.

4

| What | are | she? |
| Who | is | they? |

Q _____

A They are my grandparents.

Unit 21   It is under the tree.

Step 1 **Look and write** *in, on,* **or** *under.*

① ② ③ ④

1 The fish is _____in_____ the bowl.

2 The balls are _____ the chair.

3 The rocket is _____ the book.

4 The mouse is _____ the hole.

Step 2 **Look, choose, and write.**

| it | they | | in | on | under |

1 Where are the gifts?

_____They_____ are _____under_____ the tree.

2 Where are the cats?

_____ are _____ the basket.

3 Where is the dog?

_____ is _____ the desk.

4 Where is the cat?

_____ is _____ the box.

Unscramble and write the sentences.

1   is   the chair   under   .   The cat

→ The cat is under the chair.

2   on   is   .   The mouse   the cheese

→ _____

3   .   The hamster   in   the house   is

→ _____

4   the basket   in   are   The apples   .

→ _____

5   .   The birds   the box   are   under

→ _____

Step 1 ► **Look, choose, and write.**

① ② ③ ④

who   under   in   what

1 ____Who____ is she?   She is my aunt.

2 Where is the dog?   It is _____ the bag.

3 _____ are they?   They are coins.

4 Where are the ants?   They are _____ the apple.

Step 2 ► **Look and write.**

1

____What____ ____is____ ____it____ ?
It is a camera.

2
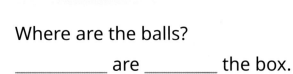

Where are the balls?
_____ are _____ the box.

3

Where is the fish?
_____ is _____ the bowl.

4

_____ _____ _____ ?
They are goats.

Unscramble and write the sentences.

1

he   Who   ?   is

Q Who is he?

A He is my friend.

2

is   ?   What   it

Q _____

A It is a guitar.

3

?   you   are   Who

Q _____

A I am a teacher.

4

.   the igloo   is   It   in

Q Where is the penguin?

A _____

5

the grass   are   .   on   They

Q Where are the kids?

A _____

Oh! My Grammar is a three-level grammar series designed for young students. *Oh! My Grammar* helps learners to easily understand basic grammar form, use, and meaning while also developing their writing skills. This series exposes students to natural English grammar so that they can learn how to use it in real-life situations. Learner-centered exercises enable students to use the grammar forms accurately and fluently. Interesting writing tasks and gradual sentence pattern practice boost students' confidence in their writing skills.

Oh! My Grammar Series

세이펜과 함께 배우는 Oh! My Grammar

<Oh! My Grammar>는 Student Book에 세이펜이 적용되어 있습니다.
세이펜을 영어에 가져다 대기만 하면 원어민의 생생한 영어 발음과 억양을 듣고 영어 말하기 연습을 할 수 있습니다.
*번역 기능 | 세이펜으로 책을 찍어서 원어민 음성을 들은 후, ⓣ 버튼을 짧게 누르면 해석 음원을 들을 수 있습니다.

🖊 세이펜을 대면 유닛명을 들을 수 있습니다. ⓣ 기능 지원

🖊 QR코드에 세이펜을 대면 해당 트랙의 MP3 파일이 재생됩니다.

🖊 세이펜을 대면 Christina 선생님의 우리말 문법 강의를 들을 수 있습니다.

🖊 그림이나 영어 단어에 세이펜을 대면 원어민의 정확한 발음과 억양을 들을 수 있습니다. ⓣ 기능 지원

🖊 세이펜을 대면 Activity의 지시문을 들을 수 있습니다. ⓣ 기능 지원

🖊 그림이나 문제에 세이펜을 대면 정답을 들을 수 있습니다. ⓣ 기능 지원

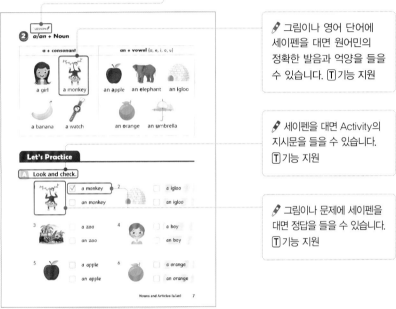

🖊 문장에 세이펜을 대면 원어민의 정확한 발음과 억양을 들을 수 있습니다. ⓣ 기능 지원

🖊 문제에 세이펜을 대면 정답이 포함된 문장을 들을 수 있습니다. ⓣ 기능 지원

🖊 그림이나 문제에 세이펜을 대면 정답이 포함된 문장을 들을 수 있습니다. ⓣ 기능 지원

🖊 세이펜을 대면 해당 영어 단어를 들을 수 있습니다. ⓣ 기능 지원

🖊 세이펜을 대면 해당 영어 문장을 들을 수 있습니다. ⓣ 기능 지원

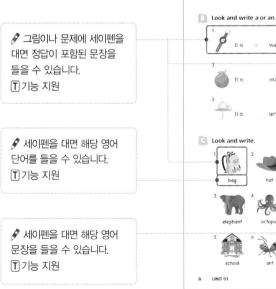

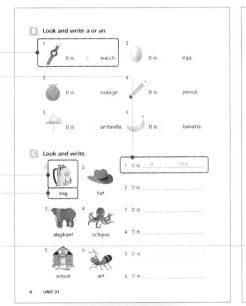

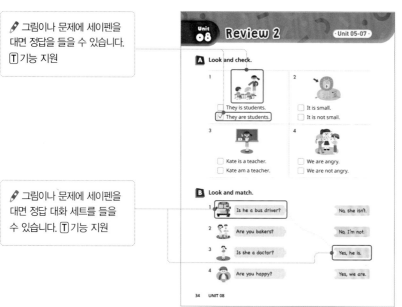

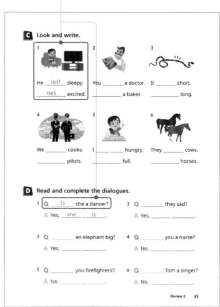

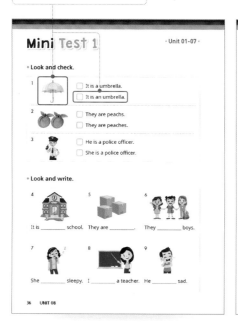

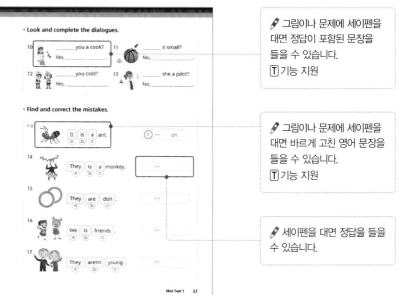